Ondřej Kanich

Fingerprint Damage Simulation

Ondřej Kanich

Fingerprint Damage Simulation

A simulation of fingerprint distortion, damaged sensor, pressure and moisture

LAP LAMBERT Academic Publishing

Impressum / Imprint

Bibliografische Information der Deutschen Nationalbibliothek: Die Deutsche Nationalbibliothek verzeichnet diese Publikation in der Deutschen Nationalbibliografie; detaillierte bibliografische Daten sind im Internet über http://dnb.d-nb.de abrufbar.

Alle in diesem Buch genannten Marken und Produktnamen unterliegen warenzeichen-, marken- oder patentrechtlichem Schutz bzw. sind Warenzeichen oder eingetragene Warenzeichen der jeweiligen Inhaber. Die Wiedergabe von Marken, Produktnamen, Gebrauchsnamen, Handelsnamen, Warenbezeichnungen u.s.w. in diesem Werk berechtigt auch ohne besondere Kennzeichnung nicht zu der Annahme, dass solche Namen im Sinne der Warenzeichen- und Markenschutzgesetzgebung als frei zu betrachten wären und daher von jedermann benutzt werden dürften.

Bibliographic information published by the Deutsche Nationalbibliothek: The Deutsche Nationalbibliothek lists this publication in the Deutsche Nationalbibliografie; detailed bibliographic data are available in the Internet at http://dnb.d-nb.de.

Any brand names and product names mentioned in this book are subject to trademark, brand or patent protection and are trademarks or registered trademarks of their respective holders. The use of brand names, product names, common names, trade names, product descriptions etc. even without a particular marking in this work is in no way to be construed to mean that such names may be regarded as unrestricted in respect of trademark and brand protection legislation and could thus be used by anyone.

Coverbild / Cover image: www.ingimage.com

Verlag / Publisher:
LAP LAMBERT Academic Publishing
ist ein Imprint der / is a trademark of
OmniScriptum GmbH & Co. KG
Heinrich-Böcking-Str. 6-8, 66121 Saarbrücken, Deutschland / Germany
Email: info@lap-publishing.com

Herstellung: siehe letzte Seite /
Printed at: see last page
ISBN: 978-3-659-63942-5

Acknowledgements

This work has been created with great help of the Faculty of Information Technology, Brno University of Technology. Specifically I would like to thank Martin Drahanský for tutoring this work. Also I want to thank to all Ph.D. students which helped me in the laboratory of biometric systems. Big thanks belong to all my friends which helped me with proofreading. Last but not least I would like to thank my family for support when this work has been created.

Contents

1 Introduction

In the last few years the fingerprint technology has moved from sci-fi movies to almost every personal device that we use. Nowadays almost every notebook has a fingerprint reader and producers of smartphones proudly advertise their new models with it as well. With the massive expansion of this technology, there are problems that emerge. More than ever there is information about someone who cracked these devices and producers of biometric systems have to react to it. As the result, there are liveness detection systems added to sensors and because of these changes, algorithms that extract features and compare them also have to change.

Sophisticated algorithms lead to larger demands on testing. This testing requires not only many fingerprints from one finger but also many fingers, that means many people involved in the testing. Capturing that many fingerprints is a very time consuming operation. When a huge amount of fingerprints is needed, it is better to use synthetic ones. There are ways to create a synthetic fingerprint. Problem with these generators is that they usually produce a perfect fingerprint without noise, scars, an unclean surface of sensor, etc. Whenever it is perfect or only slightly damaged, the synthetic fingerprint used in the recognition algorithm usually gives the right answer and that is not what is wanted. Also there are algorithms embedded to the sensors in case that a synthetic fingerprint with a sensor specific damage is required.

The main subject of this work is to describe the present technology in generating synthetic fingerprints with emphasis on the simulation of a damaged fingerprint and to design and implement methods that take the perfect fingerprint and transform it to a more realistic damaged representation. These methods take as an input different types of sensors as well as other phenomena to simulate a very specific damage done to the real fingerprint when it is scanned. This way it can not only simulate a specific damage but also generate one fingerprint exposed to different environments.

In the second chapter the current state of art is described. There is information about biometrics, the fingerprint, the process of fingerprint acquirement and sensor technologies associated with it. The third chapter is dedicated to the synthetic fingerprint and everything connected to it, i.e. way of generating the synthetic fingerprint, different data that can be as an input of the generator, current generators available and their functionality. Also phenomena that influence the real fingerprint when capturing it are described there. In the fourth chapter there can be found everything about the design of methods to simulate damage to the perfect synthetic fingerprint and the specification of elements that will be simulated. The fifth chapter deals with implementation of the designed methods, i.e. with the detailed description how the methods work, how issues with this methods were solved and how it was put all together. The sixth chapter is dedicated to the testing and the verification of the resulting synthetic fingerprints. The testing and the verification is made not only in terms of an individual damage simulation but also in terms of fingerprint image as a whole. The commercial product and the implementation of the standard of fingerprint image quality is used. The last chapter is the conclusion which sums up all the essential information.

2 State of the Art

This chapter describes the general information needed for understanding of the rest of the work. The main goal of this publication is closely related to the fingerprint used in biometrics. This first chapter is covering the basic knowledge of biometrics with the emphasis on the fingerprint and methods to acquire them. An integral part is also the way how the recognition of fingerprint works, i.e. processes that are necessary to acquire a fingerprint. All terms related to biometrics are consulted with [1].

2.1   Introduction to Biometrics

First of all what is biometrics. This term has a different meaning in information technology and in biology. Biometrics [1][2] in context of this work is an automated recognition of people based on their characteristic anatomy and behavioural features. If we think about how we can proof our electronic identity there are three basic approaches. Reveal something we know (knowledge), something we possess (possession) and something we are (biometrics). In that order the level of comfort and safety when using these approaches is raising. [2]

The main advantage of the biometric systems is that the biometric characteristic that is used to identify an individual cannot be lost or forgotten. This fact is also the greatest disadvantage of the biometric characteristic. Whenever it is revealed, there is no way to change it or delete it. Also some biometric characteristics can tell a lot about the individual health so it is violating one's privacy. [2]

There are few concepts which are important to biometrics. One is inter and intra class variability. Interclass variability tell us how big is the difference between traits from different classes (people). On the contrary, intra-class variability tell us how big the difference is between traits from the same class (individual). When we compare biometrics, there are 8 basic properties [2][3]:

- Universality, i.e. everyone should have this trait,
- Uniqueness, i.e. two persons should not have the same trait,
- Permanence, i.e. trait should not vary over time,
- Measurability, i.e. trait should be easy to acquire,
- Performance, i.e. trait should not change or age,

- Acceptability, i.e. willingness of people to capture the trait,
- Circumvention, i.e. how difficult is to make falsification,
- Price, i.e. how much it costs to deploy a biometric system with that trait.
- Maintenance, i.e. how much it costs to maintain a biometric system with that trait.

There is not a perfect biometric characteristic. Each one has its advantages and disadvantages based on these properties. [2][4]

2.2   Fingerprint

This work is mainly about the fingerprint, therefore, we should study them a little bit more deeply. Fingerprint is one of the biometric characteristics which is used to identify people since 1880. Almost a hundred years before that it was already known that fingerprints are unique. Francis Galton counted the likelihood of 2 fingerprints being the same as 1 to 64 billion. That is one of the reasons why it is one of the most widespread biometric characteristics you can see used basically in everyday life. [2]

How the fingerprint stands in comparison with other biometric characteristics? The main advantages are uniqueness, permanence, performance, circumvention and price. It is pretty decent in other characteristics too but there are better traits. One of that is acceptability. People have the fingerprint scanning very narrowly connected to the criminalistics series and films. When it comes to the scanning, many of them have inner feelings of doing something really bad. Also many of them are afraid of forgery of their fingerprints especially when it is not used to arrest some criminal element. These are a few reasons why the fingerprint doesn't have a great acceptability. Nowadays the position of the fingerprint technology is getting better and people are more willing to accept this technology because of its everyday usage. However it is still really difficult to get a fingerprint database. [2]

2.2.1   Papillary Lines

A fingerprint is created by capturing papillary lines [2][3][5] which are protrusions in the internal side of hands (and feet as well). In figure 2.1 we can see the structure of the top side of the skin. In the epidermis part there are shown some types of minutiae, which are described in the next subchapter, and sweat pores. The curvatures of papillary lines are formed in the deeper layer – the dermis. The real papillary lines

6

which we can see and capture as a fingerprint in epidermis are just a projection from the deeper layer (for example wrinkles are formed in the same layer). This means that you cannot alter or delete the fingerprint by damaging the dermis for example by burn, abrasion or cut. If you do it, it will regenerate with the grow of skin in the surface of finger. The only way to change papillary lines is by damaging the epidermis. This will permanently erase that part of papillary lines. [2][5][6]

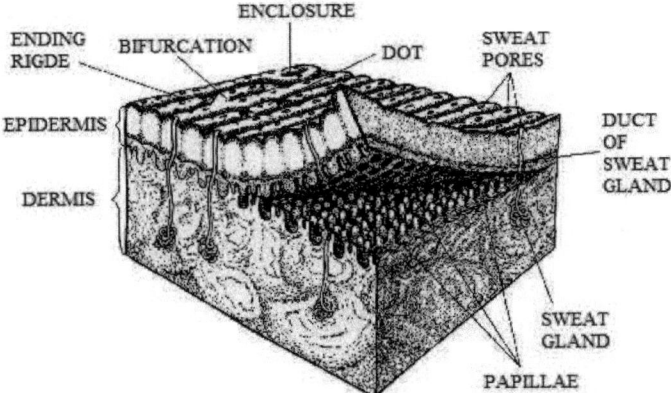

Figure 2.1: Skin Structure (taken and modified from [2]).

Papillary lines are created in the fourth month of the baby development and for the rest of the life they stay relatively the same [6]. We assume that there were no major injuries. Small injuries, wrinkles and other effects interrupt papillary lines but their continuity and minutiae will be unchanged. Papillary lines improve our sensitivity to touch and also improve our grip of objects. The height of papillary ridge is ranging from 0.1 to 0.4 millimetres and their width is around 0.2 to 0.6 millimetres. [2][6]

2.2.2 Classification of Fingerprints

The identification just by comparing two images would be a very difficult task so we divide fingerprints to certain classes. In that case we can very quickly reject fingerprints from another class, which greatly accelerates the identification. This is necessary in big databases like FBI uses. Their system IAFIS (integrated automated fingerprint identification system) [7] uses the Henry's classification system [2] which contains three classes. These are arch, loop and whorl. Nowadays, extended versions, where these three classes are split into more specific ones, are used. In figure 2.3 you can see two subclasses for every class. On the internet you can find more subclasses usually derived from the whorl class (from the arch and the loop as well). All these classes are not equally frequent in fingers. Arches are the most unique ones with the probability around 6.6%. In the middle there are whorls in 27.9% of fingers. The most frequent are loops which can be found almost two thirds of fingers (65.5%). [2][6][8]

To understand how we can distinguish these classes we need to define some concepts. The first of them is *delta* [2][3]. It is a place where papillary lines run to three different directions. It forms a triangular shape. The second of them is *core* [2][3]. Core is the centre of fingerprint and you can find it in the innermost loop or in the middle of the spiral in the whorl class. In figure Chyba: zdroj odkazu nenalezen you

Figure 2.2: Core and delta.

8

can see the core marked with blue colour and the direction of core marked with red arrow and you can also see delta marked with green triangle. Six classes in figure 2.3 all differ in quantity of cores and deltas or in the direction of cores. An arch doesn't have any cores or deltas. A tended arch has one core, one delta and a direction of core points to the delta. Loops are like the tended arch but with a different direction which specifies them. Whorls in general have two deltas and one or two cores. With all these information we can safely classify fingerprint in figure Chyba: zdroj odkazu nenalezen as a right loop. [2][3][6]

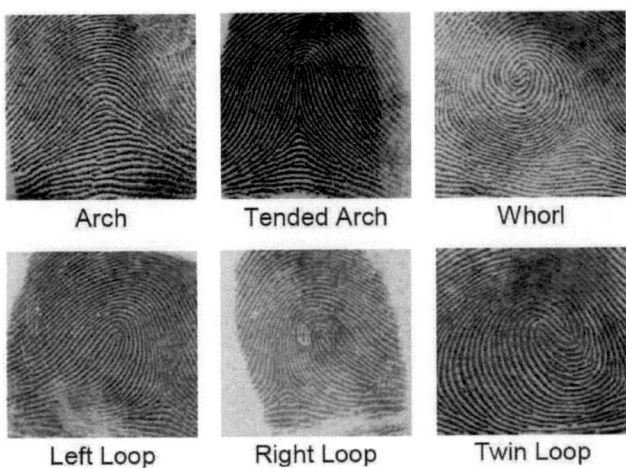

Arch   Tended Arch   Whorl

Left Loop   Right Loop   Twin Loop

Figure 2.3: Classes of fingerprints (taken and modified from [8]).

2.2.3   Fingerprint Minutiae

Only classes are not enough to identify a person. The characteristic, which is detailed enough to distinguish every finger in the world, is the fingerprint minutiae. Minutia [2] is a special formation created by papillary lines. In dactyloscopy they distinguish huge amounts of these formations. Some of them you can see in figure 2.4. From the left to the right it is [2]: ridge ending, bifurcation, double bifurcation, triple bifurcation, spur (or hook), ridge crossing, opposed bifurcation (or side contact), dot, island (short ridge), enclosure (or single whorl), double whorl, bridge, twin bridge, through line. Each type of minutia has a different likelihood of appearance in the fingerprint. [2][6][9]

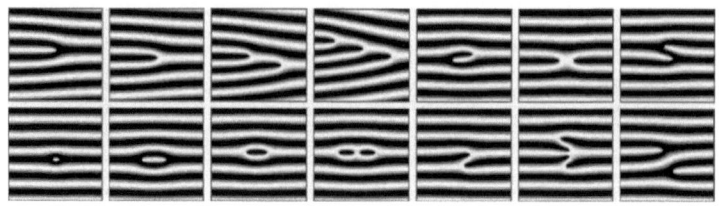

Figure 2.4: Basic types of minutiae (taken and modified from [8]).

When we use computers to recognize fingerprints and with that to find and save minutiae, it is very demanding to use all these types of minutiae. The recognition of these complicated patterns will only prolong the fingerprint acquirement. Unlike people, computers don't have problem with saving greater numbers of minutiae, their location and orientation. For these reasons computers only recognize two basic types of minutiae *ridge ending* and *bifurcation* (in figure 2.4 marked with red frame). [2][6]

2.3   Sensor Technologies for Fingerprint Acquirement

Nowadays when we use the fingerprint recognition technology, regardless of the usage (i.e. verification, identification, etc.) the first thing to do is to get a fingerprint from the finger to the computer. There are several methods of getting a digitalized fingerprint. We can scan the traditional dactyloscopic card where the fingerprint is obtained by moistening the fingertip in the ink. This method leaves our fingers dirty and there is no certainty of making a good fingerprint. It is better to have our finger scanned to the computer directly. The principle of these direct methods can be found in the next subchapters. [2][5]

Fingerprints capturing sensors are divided into the three main categories. It is sweep, contactless and touch (or area) sensors. When using touch sensors you just put the finger on the sensor area and leave it there for a few seconds without moving it. These sensors are very easy to use even for inexperienced users. The only thing that could go wrong is a bad rotation or position of the finger. The bad rotation often occurs when the thumb is being scanned (20° is usually enough for matching algorithms to stop working). People with longer fingers frequently don't estimate sensors area right and then the core of the fingerprint isn't scanned or appears in the edge of the scan which is a wrong position for many matching algorithms. The biggest disadvantage of touch sensors is that latent fingerprints can stay on them. Some technologies can get deceived by the reactivation of the last finger from latent fingerprint. A related problem to this matter is that the sensor is getting dirty with each scan and must be cleaned depending on the frequency of scanning. Dirty sensors produce dirty fingerprints which can result in a higher false reject rate [5]. A good sensor also should have the area large enough to fit everyone's finger. However, larger area means usually a higher cost. [5]

Sweeping sensors are wide approximately as a finger but their height is only a several millimetres. When using sweeping sensors you swipe your finger vertically over the sensor. The sensor will then reconstruct the fingerprint from each smaller part captured when you swiped your finger as you can see in figure 2.5. The advantage of this type of sensor is a lower price because of a much smaller area of the sensor. Also there is no latent fingerprint available (only the last part of it) and the finger movement basically cleans the sensor each time when it is used. The rotation of fingerprint is thanks to the vertical movement almost non-existent. On the other hand, the sensor is hard to use. You need several trials to get used to it. There are many things that can go wrong when swiping your finger. You have to have the exact speed, position and steadiness of your movement. When you have a wrong speed or steadiness of your finger movement, the final image is discontinuous or unrealistically long. When you have a wrong position, the final image is simply only a half of your fingerprint. The sensor must be able to scan very quickly to allow you a suitable swiping speed. The image reconstruction is time-consuming and it is also a source of inaccuracy and errors in your fingerprint. The first sweeping sensor was used with the thermal technology, but nowadays it can be used with many different technologies. [5]

Last type of sensor is contactless one. These sensors scan your papillary lines without you touching the sensor. Usually they work in a similar way to touch sensors. Because of that there are no worries of a latent fingerprint, a dirt on the sensor, a bad speed or steadiness of the fingerprint movement. On the other hand, the device is usually around your whole finger which implies a higher cost and also a lower acceptability. The only thing that is needed is the right position of the finger in the device. That could be tricky because you have to align your finger in three dimensions.

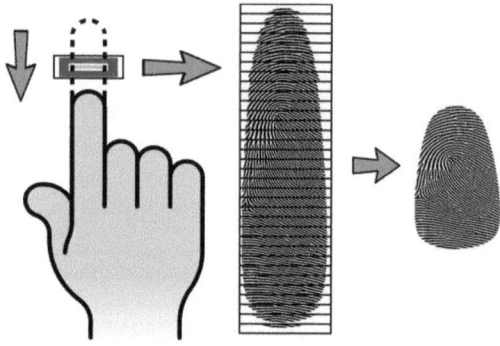

Figure 2.5: Sweeping sensor principle.

2.3.1   Optical Technology

Optical fingerprint capture devices are one of the oldest, they existed already in 1970s. They are based on Frustrated Total Internal Reflection (FTIR) [5] principle. Figure 2.6 shows us this technology in detail. The finger is placed at the protective glass so that ridges touch the glass and valleys are in the distance. The ray from the light source is reflected by the ridges and absorbed (scattered) at the valleys. The reflected rays are channelled through the optics to CCD or CMOS camera. The protective glass is illuminated by the light source like we see in 2.6. Some optical

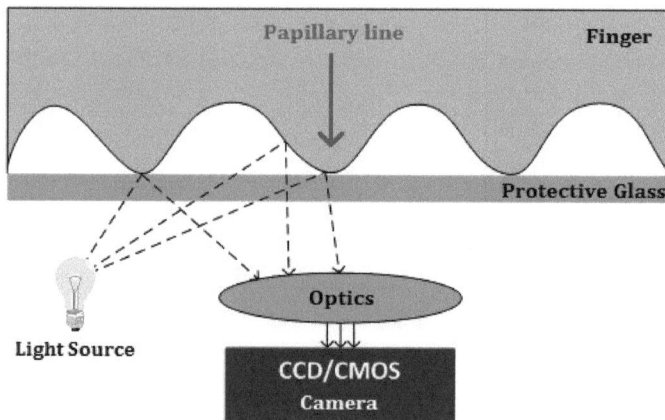

Figure 2.6: Optical technology principle (taken and modified from [8]).

12

devices use contactless technology. These devices work very similarly to primitive photographic devices. Advantages of this technology are that sensors can withstand temperature fluctuations. They operate basically in 3D so they are more resistant to photograph or fingerprint image attacks. Disadvantages are that the sensor is sensitive to dirty fingers and that latent fingerprints are still a big problem with the exception of contactless devices. [2][5]

2.3.2   Capacitive Technology

The capacitive sensor is created by a two dimensional array of micro-capacitors plate. Ridges and valleys create the second part of these micro-capacitors. In figure 2.7 we can see the difference between distances of a ridge and a valley and because of that capacitors have another electrical behaviour which can be measured. The capacitive technology capturing devices are being used widely for example as sweeping sensors in great numbers of laptops. Despite its wide usage they have some disadvantages. There is a danger of damaging the whole device when your finger is electrostatically charged. Also in perspiration there are chemicals that can damage the silicon chip. For these purposes there has to be a protective layer, but this layer has to be as thin as possible to have the smallest impact on the measurement of differences between ridges and valleys. [2][5]

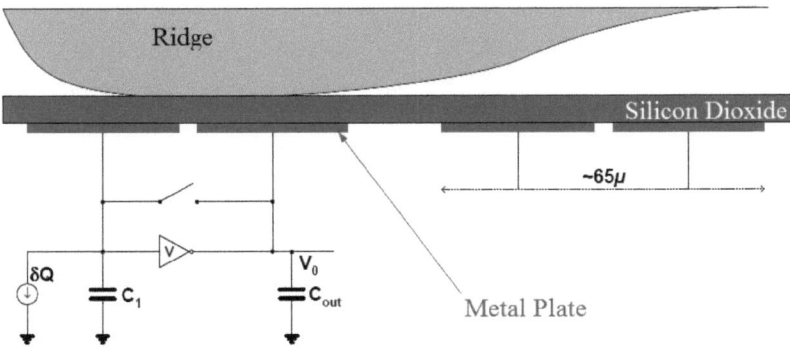

Figure 2.7: Capacitive technology principle [8].

2.3.3 Thermal Technology

Thermal technology is based on a different thermal radiation. Pyroeletric materials generate current according to various temperatures. Ridges have higher thermal radiation than valleys so they have higher temperature. Since temperatures quickly equalize, it is necessary to use sweeping sensors, see figure 2.8. The main advantage of the thermal technology is that it is very resistant to electrostatic discharge. Also the protective layer can be very thick. [2][5]

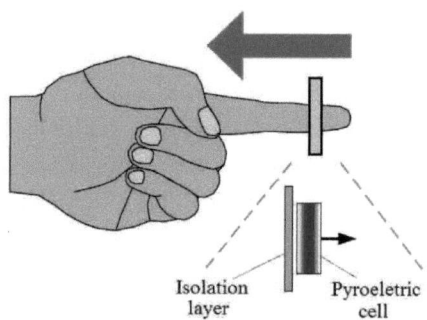

Figure 2.8: Thermal technology principle

[8].

2.3.4 Ultrasonic Technology

Ultrasonic technology capturing devices consist of a transmitter and a receiver. The transmitter sends acoustic signals which are reflected by ridges (skin) and valleys (air) differently. The transmitter and the receiver move around the finger as it is shown in figure 2.9. The receiver than receives echo signals and thanks to a different acoustic impedance measures distance and consequently acquires an image of fingerprint. The frequency used by these sensors is between 20 kHz and several GHz. Higher frequencies are helping to get higher resolution. Ultrasonic sensors have one of the best image quality and accuracy rates (10 times better than any other technology). The ultrasonic technology is penetrating the upper part of skin which results in better detection of fake fingers and also it is less influenced by the dirt on fingers (not excepting cuts) or sensors. The main disadvantages are a very high cost and the large size of the device. Another problem is also that the ultrasonic technology cannot operate properly at low temperatures. [2][5]

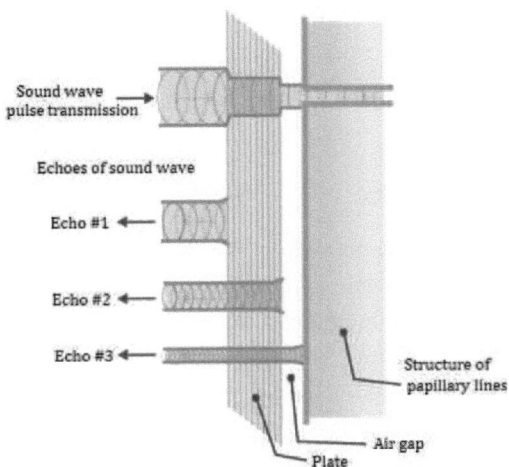

Figure 2.9: Ultrasonic technology sensor movement (taken and modified from [8]).

2.3.5　Pressure Sensitive Technology

The pressure sensitive (or piezoelectric) sensor is composed of three layers. There is a non-conductive gel added between the electroconductive layers. The whole sensor with finger ready to scan is shown in figure 2.10. The non-conductive gel is pressed by finger ridges which causes the electro conductive layers to touch. The sensor then

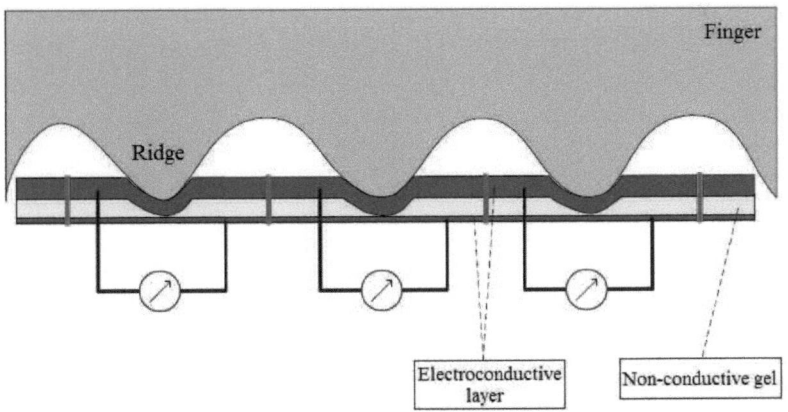

Figure 2.10: Pressure sensitive technology principle [8].

only measures the current created by the finger and creates an image of fingerprint from it. The protective layer creates a blur on the whole fingerprint. Also materials have to be sufficiently sensitive to detect the differences between valleys and ridges. [2][5][3]

2.3.6   E-field Technology

In this technology the sensor consists of a drive ring and a matrix of antennas. The drive ring generates a sinusoidal radio frequency signal and the matrix of active antennas receives that signal modulated by the skin structure, or more precisely modulated by the dermis structure, because the electric field passed the upper parts of the skin (the epidermis). Similarly to the ultrasonic technology, this technology is also resistant to fake fingers and ignores the dirt and light injuries on the finger. The image quality here is better than the one from capacitive or electro-optical sensors. The disadvantage is that the sensor is very sensitive to electrostatic charges and there is a possibility of a sensitivity to disturbance in its RF modulation. [5][3]

2.3.7   Electro-Optical Technology

The electro-optical sensor consists of 4 layers which are clearly shown in figure 2.11. It is an isolation layer, a black coaxial layer, a light emitting layer and a basic layer. Underneath there is a CCD/CMOS camera. The light emitting layer is made from a polymer which emits light when polarized with a proper voltage. When ridges touch the sensor it causes the black coaxial layer to touch the phosphor layer which then emits light in places of ridges. This light passes the basic layer and then a camera captures it. [2][5][3]

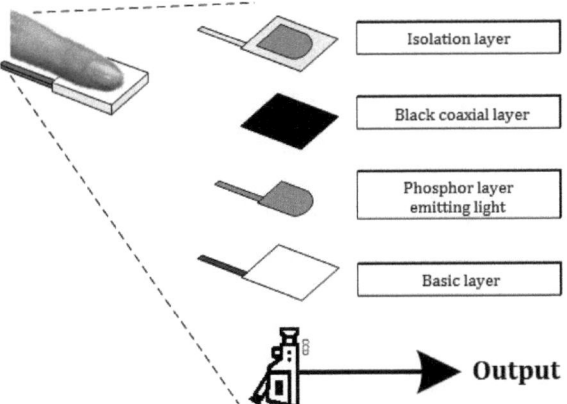

Figure 2.11: Electro-optical technology principle (taken and modified from [8]).

2.3.8 MEMS Technology

The MEMS (Micro-Electro-Mechanical-System) [5] uses micro parts to scan a fingerprint. One of the methods is using piezoresistive micro beams. The user sweeps his finger along the sensor which consists of three rows of piezoresistive gauges. Their parallel deflection will create a voltage variation which is measured and transformed into the fingerprint. Another method is using micro-heaters. This method heats finger a little bit and measures the change of temperature of the heat element. A ridge works as a heat sink so the heat element which is connected to the ridge shows a less temperature raise. [5][3]

2.4   Fingerprint Recognition Process

Now we know how to get a digitized fingerprints but there is still one process to explain - the process of recognising a fingerprint. In figure 2.12 we can see an overview of this process. First, we need a digitalized image of fingerprint. How to get them is discussed in chapter 2.3. Sensors nowadays tend to have liveness detection as a part of the scanning. [2][5]

The next phase is enhancing image quality. In each point of image including his surroundings the direction of a papillary line is counted. If this point is on the papillary line, it determines with a high probability the direction of it. This phase can be divided into smaller ones – orientation field estimation for each point, block orientation field estimation and then the final mapping on the original image. With this information the image is enhanced. In this step many various methods can be applied on the picture. Usually the method for adjusting histogram is used. Image quality enhancements are used like the Gabor filter, frequency filters (after using FFT) like the Butterworth filter or the Ikonomopoulos filter, etc. (after the application of filter IFFT is used). [2]

The next step is binarization. It is usually done by some thresholding method, e.g. by regional average thresholding or by adaptive thresholding. At the end of this step we have a binary image, where ridges are black and valleys white. [2][5]

At the end of this process we need to detect minutiae and for this purpose we need only ridges. So in this step the ridges are thinned to be only 1 pixel wide. The only problem is that the ridges shouldn't decline in any direction – that could cause a problem with minutiae position. [2]

The last phase is minutiae detection and extraction. Specialized algorithms are used for this purpose. One of them is the Hong method [2]. In this phase minutiae are detected (in verification systems usually only ridge ending and bifurcation) and its properties (position, type and gradient) are extracted. [2][5]

Fingerprint Acquirement   Image Enhancement   Binarization   Thinned Lines   Minutiae Extraction

Figure 2.12: An overview of fingerprint recognition process (taken and modified from [8]).

3 Synthetic Fingerprint

The fingerprint recognition technology is used more and more often. Along with it many methods come that make the fingerprint recognition more resistant to impostors. The amount of various recognition algorithms is greater too. These algorithms need testing and they are usually tested on small databases. Larger databases (we speak of databases with thousands or better ten thousands of fingerprints) are very hard to get because making them is very time and money demanding. It has to be a very trusted organization that tries to collect a database like that because people tend not to give their fingerprint to everyone. Collecting such a database is also very tiresome for the technician and the users. In this monotonous environment it is easy to make a mistake. Even when such a large database is available, there are usually problems with sharing it because of privacy legislations that protect these types of data. When these databases aren't available, algorithms are tested on smaller databases and it is very easy to make them data dependent. So they are very accurate when it comes to a common fingerprint (e.g. loop class) but with an extraordinary fingerprint (like twin loop class) their accuracy is falling apart. [3]

In these cases it would be great to have some generator which would create a large synthetic fingerprint database. If a synthetic database consists of images very similar to human fingerprints, than it can be used instead of a large database of real fingerprints. It also opens space for testing of just one kind of fingerprint or generating fingerprints in very bad conditions to adapt algorithms to their expected workplace. Generating such a database would save a lot of resources (human, money, time) that can be used to create better algorithms. So this is the motivation for creating synthetic fingerprints. [3]

3.1   Methods for Generating Synthetic Fingerprint

The synthetic fingerprint generation is an inverse biometrics problem. According to input variables you basically do the fingerprint recognition process (chapter 2.4) from the end to the start. There can be found several methods how to generate a synthetic fingerprint [6][9][10]. When we thoroughly study them, we can find that they are all based on the same principle. The method used by the SFinGe seems to be the oldest one and also the most commonly known so it will be described as a pattern for others.

For better understanding you can look at the upper part in figure 3.1 to see the process of the generation. The generating part ends with the so called master fingerprint (a perfect fingerprint, equivalent of phase extracted lines from figure 2.12). Firstly, the fingerprint shape is determined. The basic shape is oval and each elliptical segment can be changed to create the required shape. The second step is the directional field model. In this step the fingerprint class is chosen and together with that the position of cores and deltas. This step is using the Sherlock and Monroe ridge [3] flow model to generate a consistent direction field. The third step creates the density map. When we look at a fingerprint, we can find that the density of papillary lines isn't the same throughout the whole area. After examining several real fingerprints some heuristic criteria are made. These criteria are based on the position of singularities (cores and deltas) and according to them the density map is generated. The last step is ridge pattern generating. This phase uses all previous steps and some initial seeds. Iteratively, the image with initial seeds is refined with the Gabor filter. The filter orientation and frequency is adjusted according to the directional field and density map. Minutiae are automatically generated at random places with random types (dactyloscopic ones, not only ridge ending and bifurcation). After that phase, the master fingerprint is done. [6][9][10]

As we can see, the SFinGe generating process isn't exactly an inverted recognition process. When we strictly follow this process, we do the so called fingerprint reconstruction. These are the methods that focus on the creation of the whole fingerprint only from minutiae saved as a template in fingerprint recognition. Another method is between these two. It says that fingerprint features are dependent on each other [9]. It is following the same scheme but with dependencies on other steps. The orientation field is influenced by singular points. The minutiae density is higher around singularities and also their appearance isn't random but it is statistically driven. The minutiae direction is also dependent on their types and on the orientation of ridges around. This method firstly determines singular points, after that the orientation field and lastly the minutiae. Each step is dependent on the previous one. After all the steps the master fingerprint is made with the use of the AM-FM method. [9]

The last method uses minutiae as an input. The creation of the whole fingerprint is based only on these minutiae. The biggest difference is that the orientation field is generated from minutiae and not from classes or singular points as it was in the previous methods. It is generated from the minutiae direction and each minutia has a weight based on the distance of it from the point where we are determining the orientation field. The disadvantage of this method is that the final fingerprint could have a class that does not exist in the real world. The density map can be manually changed in this method. The default state is the uniform density map. After that, with using a similar method of Gabor filter like in SFinGe, master fingerprint is generated. Note that instead of initial seeds this method uses minutiae as these seeds and the generation starts with them so the precisely defined minutiae don't change in the process of generation. [6]

3.2   Phenomena Influencing Fingerprint

This chapter tries to sum up all the phenomena that can influence a fingerprint. This information is needed to fully revert from the final stage of the extracted lines phase to the acquired fingerprint phase. There are the three main groups of phenomena damaging the quality of fingerprint. It is finger condition, sensor condition and environment. At first influencing factors connected to the user and his finger will be described.

Almost all fingerprint scanners are influenced by the **dirt on the finger**, be it a small particle, a few grains of dust or just a greasy finger. Conductive materials and liquids are usually the most problematic types of dirt. Only ultrasonic, contactless and e-field technologies are resistant to this type of damage. **Dry or moist finger** is one of the most typical cases of damage done to a fingerprint. Whether it is because we wash our hands or we are nervous and our fingers are sweating or on the other hand we have very dry hands because of some lotion, our skin resistance can increase or decrease ten times the normal value. This usually plays a huge role in the recognition by optical, capacitive and e-field sensors. **Physical damage of a finger** like cuts or abrasions is obviously damaging the fingerprint. If it isn't a deep wound that influences papillary lines forever, there are ultrasonic and e-field technologies that scan the finger in the deeper dermis layer where the fingerprint is undamaged. There are many **skin diseases** but it is hard to tell how many people are affected by these. There are skin diseases which are changing papillary lines. In these cases only the ultrasonic and the e-field technology can reconstruct the original fingerprint from that user. And if the disease is severe enough to damage the dermis structure of papillary lines there is no way of getting the original structure. **Pressure** can turn the fingerprint into a big black oval. Only contactless sensors are fully immune to the damage that the pressure can make. In these categories there are contactless, optical, ultrasonic and e-field technologies. The change of pressure, a very big or a very low pressure or moving is also considered being part of the next category non-cooperative behaviour. All these activities lead to a very thick or thin and blurred images. **Non-cooperative behaviour of the user** is typical when the user hates biometric technology or simply tries to find the limits of its functionality. The user usually uses an unexpected pressure, moves when the device is scanning and/or places the finger in a wrong place or a wrong rotation. None of the technologies is fully resistant to these types of behaviour. [5][11]

Second, factors connected to the sensor will be described. **Dirt on the surface** has the same effects like the dirt on the finger. The problem is that it is affecting everyone who is using that device. So in the registration phase it can create a common error for every user and there is a danger that these users will not be able to be identified after cleaning up the device. In addition to fingers there are more types of dirt than can pollute the sensor area: for example metallic dust, wooden dust, earth dust, fine sand, excrements (in outdoor use). These could be on fingers too but there are easily pictured on the sensor. In addition to ultrasonic and e-field technologies, every sweep sensor is also more resistant to this type of damage. **Latent fingerprint** is closely related to the previous topic. It is in some way a type of dirt on the surface of the sensor. More than damaging a new fingerprint there is a security hazard. These fingerprints can be copied or reactivated to breach the biometric device. The technologies, which are resistant to latent fingerprint, are the same like those in the previous topic. **Physical damage** is an extreme but a possible influencing factor of the resulting fingerprint. There is no easy way to prevent the sensor from damaging. The damage of the sensor will have different effects on every technology. In the optical technology, for example, the glass crack could be seen in the fingerprint. [5][11]

The last type of influencing factors is the surrounding environment. **Vibration** in some degree is not a problem, but when the vibrations are large, they can unfasten some internal components causing the device to break down. In another situation they can slightly change the position of finger. This movement, as it was described in the user influencing factors, can blur the fingerprint. Only sensors using the sweep technology are to a certain degree resistant to this type of damage. **Temperature** can be different for the sensor, the finger or the environment. Typically there are no problems with the exception of the thermal technology. But when we think about extreme temperatures, we have to deal with very dry or very moist fingers which can affect the resulting image. Also it is known that the ultrasonic technology doesn't operate properly in extremely low temperatures. **Surrounding light** is only affecting optical and electro-optical technologies because they have a light sensing unit. Usually to keep the cost of the sensor low the sensor area is small so that the finger covers it. In that case there is no problem with the surrounding light. However, when the sensor area is larger, the finger of the user is smaller, a smaller finger like a pinkie is used or the contactless technology is used, the influence of the surrounding light can be huge. **Electro-magnetic radiation** is an influencing factor which affects every technology. The device as a whole can be influenced by electro-magnetic radiation. Wires inside or outside connecting it to other parts of biometric system and all electronic components can be influenced. Some devices for example will create a blurred image. [5][11]

3.3 SFinGe

SFinGe (Synthetic Fingerprint Generator) [12] is an application for the synthetic fingerprint generation implemented at University of Bologna. It is currently in 4.1st version. The fingerprint database generated from different versions of SFinGe was one of the four databases of FVC (Fingerprint Verification Contest) [3]. In each year (2000, 2002, 2004 and 2006) contestants had similar results in synthetic database and real fingerprint databases. This implies that SFinGe has the inter-class and intra-class variation of synthetic fingerprint very similar to real ones. [12]

The process of the fingerprint generation is shown in figure 3.1. The upper part, i.e. the part that ends with the generated master fingerprint, is described in the subchapter 3.1. For more real looking fingerprint certain damage simulation methods are applied. These are in the lower part of figure 3.1. The first step is the selection of the contact region. To simulate the different placements of the finger on the sensor area a random translation of the ridge pattern is made. This is done without modifying the global fingerprint shape and position. The next step is the variation in ridge thickness. The ridge thickness is modified to simulate various skin dampness and finger pressure. Wet skin and higher pressure cause ridges to appear thicker and in that case the erosion operator is used. Dry skin and lower pressure make ridges thinner so in this case the dilatation operator is needed. A randomly selected magnitude of dampness and pressure determines which square box will be used and also which of the morphological operators will be used. The next phase is the fingerprint distortion. In this phase the skin deformation according to different finger placements over the sensor is simulated. The skin plasticity (compression or stretching) and a different force applied on each part of the finger creates a non-linear distortion. For this distortion Lagrangian interpolation is used. The next step is noising and rendering. In this step many small factors are simulated. Unfortunately these small factors are damaging fingerprint the most. These include irregularity of the ridges, non-uniform pressure of the finger, different contact of ridges with the sensor, presence of small pores and other noise. The noise is generated in four substeps. Firstly, valleys (or white pixels) are separately saved. Secondly, the noise in form of various stains is added. Thirdly, the whole image is smoothed with 3 times 3 windows. Lastly, valleys saved in the first step are returned back to the image (to prevent excessive smoothing in the third step). Another phase is the global translation or rotation. This phase simulates the not perfectly placed finger on the sensor. So it slightly translates and/or rotates the whole image. The last step is the generation of a realistic background. The background is generated randomly from a set of background images and the mathematical method based on KL transform which will create new backgrounds from these that are in the set of backgrounds. At the end of that step the fingerprint impression is made. For the generation of databases there are several impressions made from one master fingerprint. [9][3][10][13]

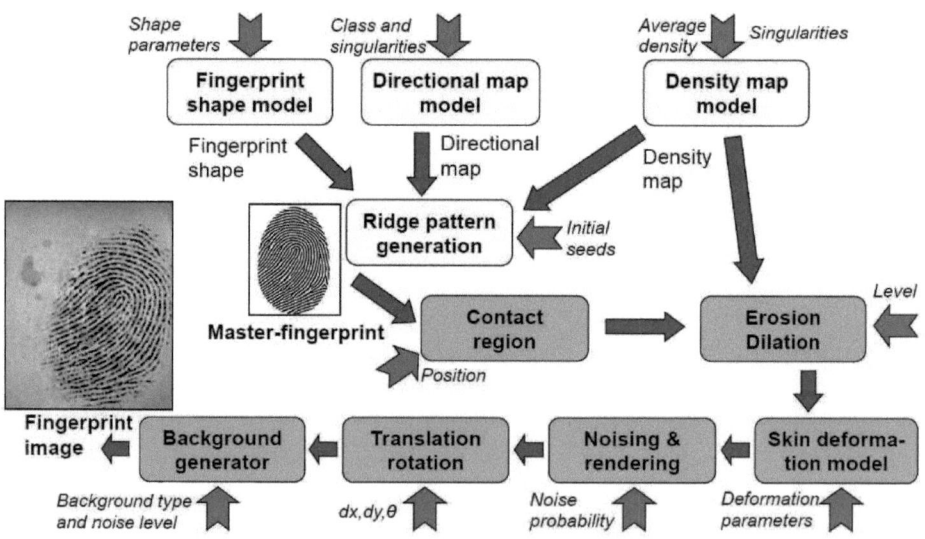

Figure 3.1: SFinGe process of fingerprint generation (taken from [10]).

4 Design of Methods to Create a Damaged Fingerprint

As could be found in chapter 3.2 damaging a fingerprint is an inverse process from the final stage of extracted lines from figure 2.12 to the stage fingerprint acquirement in the same figure. Processes that lead to this phase are binarization, orientation field estimation and image enhancement. The detailed description is in the subchapter 2.4. Unfortunately even the last step, the binarization phase, is irreversible and is cleaning much of the different damage that was done to the fingerprint. Because of this the simulation of damage done to the fingerprint cannot be just an inverted operation to the fingerprint recognition process. It is fair to say that many methods used in fingerprint recognition can be used in simulation of damage whether edited or as an inverse method.

In the chapter 3.2 we also learnt about many influencing factors that damage the fingerprint. It is hard to see how the damaged fingerprint really looks like. Databases which are created usually for the recognition algorithm testing do not contain a lot of damaged fingerprints. These fingerprints are deleted as wrongly scanned ones. The biggest clues how damaged fingerprints really look like give me the scanning sessions which I attend. During several days a fingerprint database was created. In this work only some of influencing factors are chosen to be simulated. Based on the observations that were made during the scanning sessions and after the consultation with my supervisor some influencing factors were chosen. In the next subchapters, the chosen phenomena are described. There is also information why they were chosen and what methods can simulate them.

These factors are applicable to several types of sensors. For generalization they are labelled as general sensors because all damage would have a very similar effect on optical and capacitive sensors that are currently the most used types of sensors. Also the damage simulations are restricted to touch sensors.

All these damage simulations must be held in one clean interface. To do that it is essential to use the modular approach on this interface. The information about sensor, type of sensor, damage and all controls related to it has to be easily readable. There is also a possibility that more damage simulations or sensors will be added to this application so the interface has to be ready for it. The interface should also allow us to do basic operations with the fingerprint image e.g. load a prearranged synthetic fingerprint image, save the current image. Saving and loading should use standard image formats.

4.1 Damaged Sensor

I will start with the damaged sensor simulation. There are databases (specifically with the optical sensor) in which this type of damage is clearly shown. It is a thin black line usually connected to the edge of the acquired fingerprint. This line corresponds with the crack on the protective glass. In extreme cases there could be a web of broken glass instead of this one crack. Some types of dirt on the sensor look like this crack. For example an eyelash of straight hair leaves the same trace on the acquired fingerprint. This phenomenon was also listed in chapter 3.2.

It will be simulated by simply drawing a line in the desired area on the fingerprint. It is necessary to find the right thickness of the line to properly simulate the crackle or hair on the sensor. This method and the damage simulation was chosen because of the clear impact on the fingerprint and a relative simplicity. These two features made this simulation perfect for testing the interface. Also in extreme cases they both can be done intentionally by the user. This method is required to be fully determined by a starting point, a direction and a length.

4.2 Pressure and Moisture

When it comes to applying an intentional damage to the fingerprint, too much pressure is the first thing that comes to mind. That is the main reason why it was chosen. Similarly like in the simulation of a damaged sensor, moisture influences the final image in the same way as pressure. Both dampness and pressure increase the thickness and the contrast of the ridges. The more pressure the user applies or the damper his finger is, the more thick the lines are. In extreme cases almost no lines are visible on the fingerprint because the fingerprint is either entirely black or white. This factor was also mentioned in chapter 3.2.

Morphological operations erosion and dilation [14] will be used to simulate these effects. These operators are commonly used in image processing for example to increase readability of the text or thinning the lines as in the same part of the fingerprint recognition process (chapter 2.4). They are defined and used only on binary-coloured or greyscale images. Applying the pressure does the same thing as morphological operators which enlarge or shrink papillary lines. Morphological operators need only a structure element to determine their magnitude.

4.3   Fingerprint Distortion

Fingerprint distortion is the only simulated damage that is typically done unintentionally. This type of damage is so common that it is almost impossible to made a fingerprint image without it. It is created due to the skin deformation and the non-orthogonal finger pressure to the sensor. In fact every little finger movement when touching the sensor glass is creating this distortion. Our skin is very elastic and except for extreme cases we do not even feel it. To make a non-distorted image we have to really concentrate on not moving our finger and applying the pressure exactly orthogonally. Even this could not be enough because we are creating two dimensional images out of a three dimensional finger so the skin is stretching and compressing and thus creating distortion just by this fact. The fingerprint distortion is one of the few damages that can change the position of minutia and even change the distance among minutiae themselves. This is a problem for fingerprint recognition algorithms that use the minutiae position as one of the main recognition elements. Despite that fact the distortion is almost invisible to an untrained eye. Specialized images with marked minutiae or using square grid are necessary. In chapter 3.2 the non-

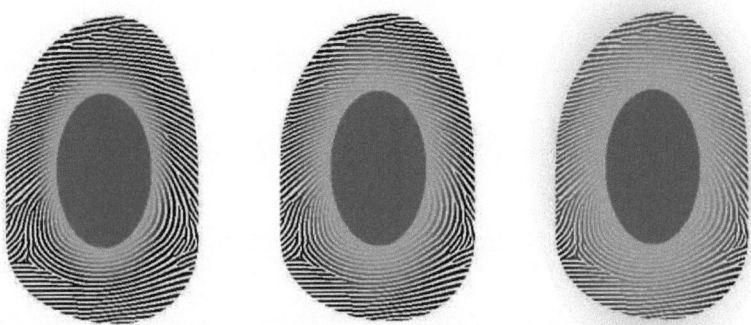

Figure 4.1: Various fingerprint distortion areas.

cooperative behaviour of the user is described. If the user is forced to enroll his fingerprints or wants to inconspicuously damage the fingerprint by small movements and changes of pressure, it leads to this distortion.

The same distortion model as in SFinGe will be used to simulate this distortion. In [15] they design a model and also verify it. The model divides the fingerprint into three areas (as you can see in figure 4.1). It is the internal area (shown by red colour) where finger is pushed so hard that the skin cannot be deformed. The second is the external area (shown by yellow colour) where the pressure is so low that the skin is maximally distorted. And the third area is transition area (shown by orange colour) which combines the two previous areas. The greater the intensity of orange colour shown is, the lower distortion is applied. Each image in figure 4.1 shows different level of skin plasticity set. After this the angle and the translation in each axis are needed to fully determine and apply the distortion. Because it can be made worst by intentionally trying to achieve this type of damage, the range of input values was increased to cover these cases.

5 Implementation of the Designed Methods

The first decision before the implementation can start is what language we should use. As it was described in chapter 4 we need a graphical user interface and we need strictly modular approaches which only object oriented languages can ensure. Even with these constraints there are many options: C++ with Qt, C#, Java and so on. Before we can damage a synthetic fingerprint we need one to work with. For this purpose it was decided to use the Chaloupka's fingerprint generator [6]. It generates a master fingerprint from minutiae as it was covered in chapter 3.1. It uses C# language and that solves the puzzle which language to use. With this language it is possible to merge the Chaloupka's fingerprint generator and the damage simulations to one application that can then generate damaged synthetic fingerprints.

5.1   Graphical User Interface

As it was described in chapter 4 a clear GUI (graphical user interface) which will not block a further extension of application is needed. The starting point was the existing Chaloupka's generating window. It is full of information and options to generate a new synthetic fingerprint. There is not much space for extensions so the fingerprint damage simulations will be in new section. As this new section can theoretically contain all influential factors, it will be implemented as a new window, as a next step to this existing application. To sum up, before we can start the damage simulation we need information about sensor technology (chapter 2.3), sensor type (touch, sweep, contactless) and damage we are going to simulate. As it was said the number of damages is theoretically overwhelming so it will be better to divide them as it was in chapter 3.2. So the first part of the application deals with the sensor, the second with the damage and the third part is reserved for the options and input values of individual damage simulations. The last part is of course the fingerprint image that is carried on from the generating window. There also has to be a way to set dependencies among individual simulations. Some simulations need to be done in certain order to give proper results.

From this description it is obvious that sensors and damage simulations will be separate objects. To ensure a proper connection with the main application window some interface is needed. The interface is implemented as an abstract class from which concrete sensors and damage simulations are derived. Figure 5.1 represents a class diagram of implemented application (that means it is without Chaloupka's classes for generation of fingerprints and first the main window). It is necessary to know that the class diagram 5.1 does not show all the fields, properties and methods (note that also parameters of methods are not listed). Next paragraphs will describe individual classes.

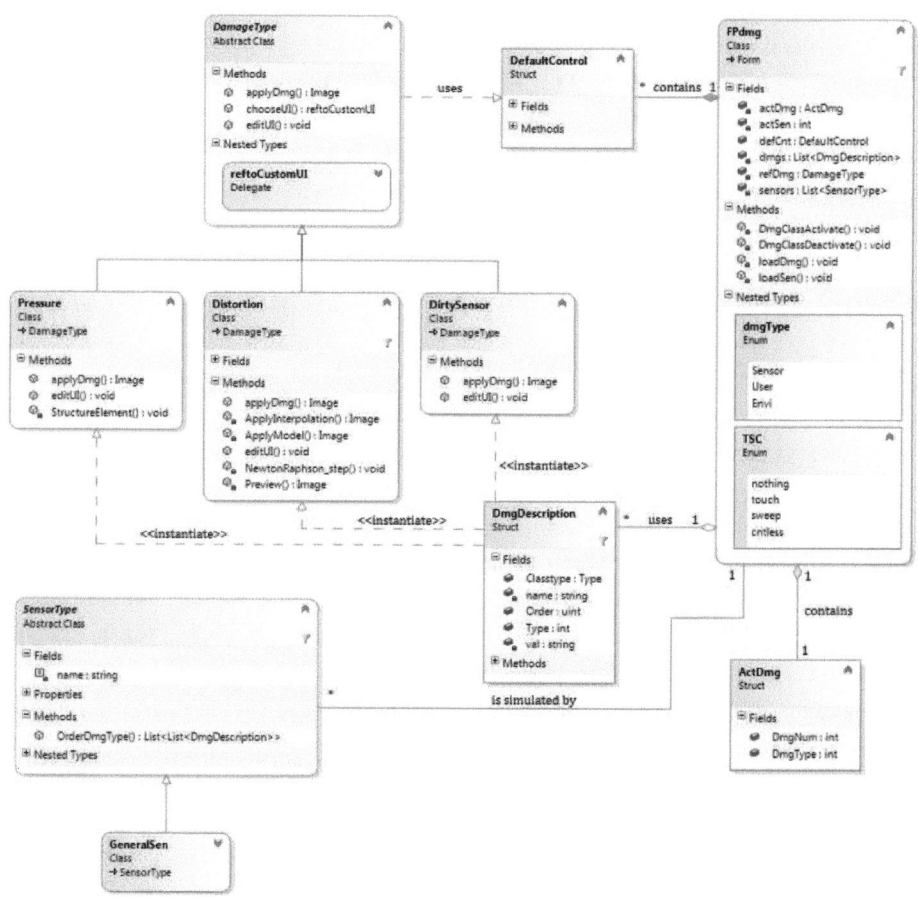

Figure 5.1: Class diagram of the application.

5.1.1   SensorType

It is an abstract class that encapsulates the sensor name, its possible types (touch, sweep or contactless) and for each type it defines an order of damage simulations. The method *OrderDmgType* orders from its own list all available damage simulations from *FPdmg* (the class of the main window or GUI) for all possible types of sensors and returns them back to *FPdmg*. When creating new sensor it is only needed to create a new class derived from *SensorType*, fill its possible types, name and order of damages and sign-up this new sensor in *loadSen* method in *FPdmg*.

5.1.2   DamageType

It is an abstract class that encapsulates methods of damaging the fingerprint, editing the default user interface and choosing whether to use its own user interface or not. With one exception all these methods take *DefaultControl* structure as a parameter. This structure contains all elements of the so called default control (see below). Method *editUI* is used to change visibility, names and range of the values, method *applyDmg* is used to take the user input. The current fingerprint image is also needed in *applyDmg* method that as the result returns a new damaged fingerprint image. To create new damage simulation it is needed to create a new class derived from *DamageType* and redefine (override) usually two of the three previous methods (chooseUI is the method to provide some support for demanding damage simulation that needs to create its own panel of controls and option in *FPdmg* so it is not usually needed to override this method). After that the new damage simulation is registered by filling out *DmgDescription* structure in *loadDmg* method of *FPdmg*.

5.1.3   FPdmg

It is the class that represents GUI and also connections to all elements. From *Form1* it takes the generated fingerprint and shows it in the picturebox on the right. GUI respects what was above, it is divided into the sensor area, the damage area and the damage simulation controls area (for better understanding see figure 5.2). Based on *loadSen* and *loadDmg* (methods that are responsible for registering all available sensors and damage simulations) it is filling GUI with appropriate sensors and damage simulations. They are also responsible for enabling and disabling currently possible sensors types and damage types (inspired by the division of influencing factors in chapter 3.2), showing respective controls for damage simulation. For easier control there are button Next and Previous which will choose and set the next or previous damage simulation (the order is identified by sorting method in given *SensorType* class). When the user clicks on the button Apply, a specific *applyDmg* method is called from the variable *refDmg*.

How exactly does the GUI know what damage class to call? In *refDmg* there is always a right derived class from *DamageType*. That is assured by the method *DmgClassActivate* with conjunction with the field *Classtype* of structure *DmgDescription*. Factory design method pattern [16] is used here. It is generally used for creating an object of a class without knowing exactly in time of compiling which class it will be. *DmgClassActivate* assigns to *refDmg* that derived *DamageType* class which is created as an instance of class from *Classtype*. This is happening every time when the user selects a specific damage. The structure *DefaultControl* is used to encapsulate all elements of the control part of GUI. That can be useful for the communication between *FPdmg* and *DamageType* classes and when adding new control element.

There are of course possibilities of loading image, saving image and clearing current image. Supported formats for these operations are bmp, png, tif, gif and jpg. As an extension basic batch processing was implemented. Many options of this batch processing are predefined. After creating a new window to set all these options (and design a new way of defining values of individual simulation) it will be perfect. The method *Batch* predefines that all images to load and save will be in the folder "batch" (where the application is executed), their name will be "SFPx" where x is the sample number, and their format will be png. It loads all available images and on each of them uses every combination of current active damage simulations with default values or values defined in *BatchDefValFiller* method.

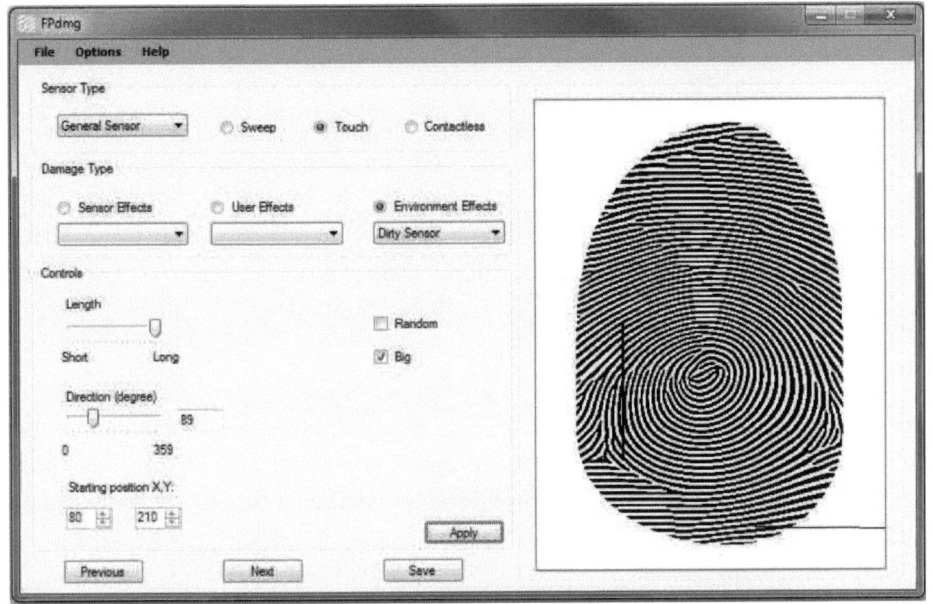

Figure 5.2: Screenshot of final GUI.

5.2   Individual Damage Simulation

In this subchapter individual damage simulations and classes that are representing them are described. It is possible to simulate some factors with one damage simulation. *Pressure*, *Distortion* and *DirtySensor* classes from diagram 5.1 will be described. Currently all classes use *DefaultControl* and the standard controls part of the user interface. In figure 5.2 we can see all standard controls, i.e. two trackbars (in figure labelled as length, direction), two checkboxes (labelled random, big) and two numerical inputs (labelled starting position x,y). The class *DirtySensor* is used for the simulation of dirt on the sensor and damaged sensor. In the following subchapters methods *applyDmg* of each respective class, i.e. exact methods of damaging of the fingerprint image, are described.

5.2.1   Damaged Sensor

The method proposed in chapter 4.1 needs these three input value: starting point, a direction and length. These are connected to GUI by two trackbars and two numerical inputs as we can see in figure 5.1. The method itself is pretty straightforward, drawing the line from the starting point to the point given by the direction and the length.   This   point   is   defined   as $x=\sin(angle)\cdot length$ and $y=\cos(angle)\cdot length$. The trackbar defines the value which is from 0 to 15 and it determines the relative length of line. The length is defined exactly as $length=\dfrac{ImageWidth}{10}\cdot(1+\dfrac{Value\cdot 2}{10})$. To draw line a method from C# library was used. As it turns out it is necessary to define also the thickness of the line. For a damaged sensor the lowest (1 pixel) thickness is appropriate, but for the dirt on the finger, e.g. hair, more is needed. For this purpose one of the checkboxes was used. The other one was used to generate all previously mentioned values randomly. So in the end all standard controls were used.

5.2.2   Pressure and Moisture Simulation

The method outlined in chapter 4.2 needs only a structure element as an input. As will be explained below, four structure elements are used and you select them on the trackbar. The method itself is defined by these formulas (where B is an input -

structure   element): $erosion(x,y)=\min_{\forall(s,t)\in B}(x+s,y+t)$

$dilatation(x,y)=\max_{\forall(s,t)\in B}(x+s,y+t)$ [14]. In image processing the image is (by image it is meant a digital image) represented by $f(x,y)=intensity$ - a function of two variables which determines what the intensity of colour is. Note that in this work only greyscale images are used so the intensity is equal to some shade of grey. The input variables x and y are coordinates of the pixel on the screen (which means that they are integers).

The structure element consists of pixels in the neighbourhood of the investigated pixel x,y. In this application it should be evenly distributed around the investigated one. After defining the smallest structure element that is evenly distributed (it was the structure element c from figure 5.3) it turns out that it has too great an impact on the fingerprint image. Because of that it was necessary to include the structure element b (from the same figure) despite the fact that its damage to fingerprint is inaccurate.

The method *StructureElement* than transforms value from the trackbar into one these five structure elements shown in figure 5.3. These elements are saved relatively from the investigated point.

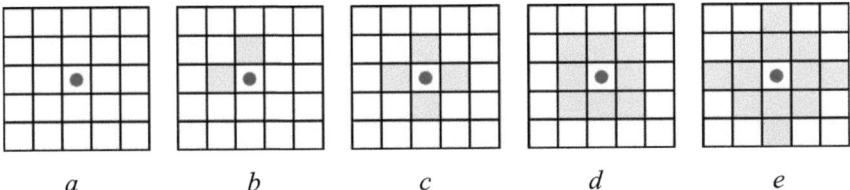

a   *b*   *c*   *d*   *e*

Figure 5.3: A demonstration of all structure elements used.

The user sets the level of dampness and/or pressure on the trackbar. If the set value is in the centre of the slider, then the structure element a is used and the result is the same image. Other values represent either erosion when damper or higher pressure is simulated or dilatation when dry or lower pressure is simulated. Distance from the equilibrium position corresponds with structure element from the left to the right in figure 5.3. When the structure element is referring to pixel which is not a part of the image, a default value is used. The default value is a white colour for erosion and a black one for dilatation.

5.2.3 Fingerprint Distortion

For this damage simulation the model from SFinGe, which was partially described in the chapter 4.3, will be used. As an input values model it needs individual areas of damage, value of translation in axis x and y and rotation angle. For an easy recognition the rotation angle will be labelled as θ, the value of translation as dx and dy. For the definition of all areas skin plasticity (labelled as sp) and ellipse defined by centre of ellipse ($ellip_x$ and $ellip_y$) and semi-axes ($semi_x$ and $semi_y$) are used. More information can be found in the next paragraphs. The method, or more precisely the distortion model, is defined by these formulas [15]:

$$distortion : \Re^2 \rightarrow \Re^2, \quad coef : \Re \times \Re \rightarrow \Re, \quad \Delta : \Re^2 \rightarrow \Re^2, \quad dist : \Re^2 \rightarrow \Re$$

$$distortion(v) = v + \Delta(v) \cdot coef(dist(v), sp) \tag{1}$$

$$coef(dist(v), sp) = \frac{1}{2}\left(1 - \cos\left(\frac{dist(v) \cdot \pi}{sp}\right)\right) \tag{2}$$

$$\Delta(\boldsymbol{v}) = \left(R_\theta(\boldsymbol{v} - \boldsymbol{ellip}) + \boldsymbol{ellip} + \boldsymbol{d} \right) - \boldsymbol{v},$$

$$\boldsymbol{d} = \begin{bmatrix} dx \\ dy \end{bmatrix}, \quad R_\theta = \begin{bmatrix} \cos\theta & \sin\theta \\ -\sin\theta & \cos\theta \end{bmatrix}, \quad \boldsymbol{ellip} = \begin{bmatrix} elip_x \\ elip_y \end{bmatrix} \qquad (3)$$

$$dist(\boldsymbol{v}) = \sqrt{(\boldsymbol{v} - \boldsymbol{ellip})^T A^{-1} (\boldsymbol{v} - \boldsymbol{ellip})} - 1, \qquad A = \begin{bmatrix} semi_x^2 & 0 \\ 0 & semi_y^2 \end{bmatrix} \qquad (4)$$

Special cases: *Area A*: $coef = 0$, $dist = 0$ *Area C*: $coef = 1$

As it was indicated, the model is not changing the intensity of pixels but it is changing their position. So each pixel $\boldsymbol{v} = \begin{bmatrix} v_x \\ v_y \end{bmatrix}$ is transformed to new coordinates $\boldsymbol{v}' = \begin{bmatrix} v_x{}' \\ v_y{}' \end{bmatrix}$ following the formula (1). At first the ellipse usage will be explained. As it was described in chapter 4.3, the model is calculating the distortion of finger when creating two dimensional images. As we can see the elevated part of fingertips on our fingers is more or less elliptical. That part is determining the individual areas which the model uses to create distortion. The shape was generalized to ellipse with the centre in the centre of the image and semi-axes values $semi_x = 60$ and $semi_y = 100$. These values were determined experimentally because there is no information about fingerprint image and there is no better way of determining them in this state. All other input values are taken from the user.

In the next paragraphs all formulas (1-4) will be explained. Although mathematical formulas listed above are very comprehensible for humans, they are not comprehensible for computer. Matrix and vector operations are usually very slow and have limited power. For these reasons most of the formulas were modified and their modified version will be shown below. Area A corresponds with the internal area from chapter 4.3 and it is represented by a defined ellipse (including boundaries). Area B corresponds with the transition area from the same chapter and it is represented by points around ellipse that are in a certain distance, i.e. a distance which must be lower or equal to skin plasticity. Finally area C is the external area and it is represented by other pixels. Areas A, B and C are shown in figure 4.1 in respective colours red, orange and yellow.

Formula (4) determines the distance of the current pixel from the nearest point of the ellipse (area A). Mahalanobis distance decreased by one is used (as it was in [15]). In the method *Dist* the formula (4) is adjusted to:

$$dist\left(\boldsymbol{v}\right)=\sqrt{\left(\boldsymbol{v}-\boldsymbol{ellip}\right)^{T}\frac{1}{semi_{x}^{2}\cdot semi_{y}^{2}}\begin{bmatrix}semi_{y}^{2} & 0 \\ 0 & semi_{x}^{2}\end{bmatrix}\left(\boldsymbol{v}-\boldsymbol{ellip}\right)}-1$$

$$dist\left(\boldsymbol{v}\right)=\sqrt{\left(\boldsymbol{v}-\boldsymbol{ellip}\right)^{T}\begin{bmatrix}semi_{x}^{-2} & 0 \\ 0 & semi_{y}^{-2}\end{bmatrix}\left(\boldsymbol{v}-\boldsymbol{ellip}\right)}-1$$

$$dist\left(\boldsymbol{v}\right)=\sqrt{\begin{bmatrix}\left(v_{x}-ellip_{x}\right)\cdot semi_{x}^{-2} \\ \left(v_{y}-ellip_{y}\right)\cdot semi_{y}^{-2}\end{bmatrix}\left(\boldsymbol{v}-\boldsymbol{ellip}\right)}-1$$

$$dist\left(\boldsymbol{v}\right)=\sqrt{\left(\left(v_{x}-ellip_{x}\right)^{2}\cdot semi_{x}^{-2}+\left(v_{y}-ellip_{y}\right)^{2}\cdot semi_{y}^{-2}\right)}-1 \qquad (5)$$

Formula (2) basically specifies where the point is (in area B) between area A and C. The coefficient effect can be seen in figure 4.1 where it is used to define the intensity of the orange colour representing area B. The formula itself remains as it is and is used in the same way as the method *Break_koef*.

Formula (3) is representing the effect of rotation and translation. It shifts the image so that it has the centre of rotation (centre of ellipse) in the coordinates $(0, 0)^{\mathrm{T}}$. Than it uses R_{θ} matrix to rotate and shift image back to original coordinates. After that it does translation by adding the respective value and subtracts the original value of the pixel to create a difference value. Adjusted formula below was used in the method *Delta*.

$$\Delta\left(v_{x}\right)=\left(\left(v_{x}-ellip_{x}\right)\ \cos\left(\theta\right)\ +\left(v_{y}-ellip_{y}\right)\sin\left(\theta\right)\right)+ellip_{x}+dx-v_{x} \qquad (6)$$

$$\Delta\left(v_{y}\right)=\left(\left(v_{x}-ellip_{x}\right)\left(-\sin\left(\theta\right)\right)+\left(v_{y}-ellip_{y}\right)\cos\left(\theta\right)\right)+ellip_{y}+dy-v_{y} \qquad (7)$$

Formula (1) puts all things together, the difference is modified by a coefficient and added to the original value. If $\underline{v}$ is in area A, it stays as it was. If $\underline{v}$ is in area C, it is maximally translated and rotated because the coef is 1. If $\underline{v}$ is in area B, it is translated and rotated to some degree depending on the accurate location. This formula corresponds to the method *Disto*.

When real fingers stretch or compress, the sensor acquires a distorted image, but when we have a perfect non-distorted image, there are limited number of points. In spots where the finger is stretching the model does not have points to distort. To fill these places interpolation is needed. Before we can properly use interpolation we need to find out the undistorted coordinates of each pixel we want to interpolate. That means we need to compute the inversion model. This is complicated because this model cannot be analytically inverted. To determine its inverted value we need to use a numerical method. For this model the Newton-Raphson method, which can compute numerically the inversion of multiple variable functions, was used. Its variant for two variables can be written as [17][18]:

$$\begin{bmatrix} x_{i+1} \\ y_{i+1} \end{bmatrix} = \begin{bmatrix} x_i \\ y_i \end{bmatrix} - [J]^{-1} \cdot \begin{bmatrix} f_1(x) \\ f_2(x) \end{bmatrix} \quad where \quad x = \begin{bmatrix} x_i \\ y_i \end{bmatrix}, \quad J = \begin{bmatrix} \dfrac{\partial f_1(x)}{\partial x} & \dfrac{\partial f_1(x)}{\partial y} \\ \dfrac{\partial f_2(x)}{\partial x} & \dfrac{\partial f_2(x)}{\partial y} \end{bmatrix} \tag{8}$$

Now it is necessary to prepare the formula (1) representing the model to use in the formula (8). As we can see we need two functions. We get them by adjusting the formula (1) to not use vectors:

$$disto_x(v) = v_x + \Delta(v_x) \cdot coef(dist(v), sp) \tag{9}$$
$$disto_y(v) = v_y + \Delta(v_y) \cdot coef(dist(v), sp) \tag{10}$$

After that we put the formulas (9) and (10) to the formula (8) and we get:

$$\begin{bmatrix} v_{x(i+1)} \\ v_{y(i+1)} \end{bmatrix} = \begin{bmatrix} v_{x(i)} \\ v_{y(i)} \end{bmatrix} - [J]^{-1} \cdot \begin{bmatrix} disto_x(v) \\ disto_y(v) \end{bmatrix}$$

$$where \quad v = \begin{bmatrix} v_{x(i)} \\ v_{y(i)} \end{bmatrix}, \quad J = \begin{bmatrix} \dfrac{\partial disto_x(v)}{\partial v_x} & \dfrac{\partial disto_x(v)}{\partial v_y} \\ \dfrac{\partial disto_y(v)}{\partial v_x} & \dfrac{\partial disto_y(v)}{\partial v_y} \end{bmatrix} \tag{11}$$

A further modification will be divided by area where current $\underline{x}$ is located. When $\underline{x}$ is in area A, there is no distortion so points are the same as in the original picture and no interpolation nor distortion is needed to compute. If $\underline{x}$ is in area C, it means that the coefficient is equal to one and the Jacobian matrix J_C for area C will be:

$$J_C = \begin{bmatrix} \dfrac{\partial v_x}{\partial v_x} + \dfrac{\partial \Delta(v_x)}{\partial v_x} & \dfrac{\partial v_x}{\partial v_y} + \dfrac{\partial \Delta(v_x)}{\partial v_y} \\ \dfrac{\partial v_y}{\partial v_x} + \dfrac{\partial \Delta(v_y)}{\partial v_x} & \dfrac{\partial v_y}{\partial v_y} + \dfrac{\partial \Delta(v_y)}{\partial v_y} \end{bmatrix}$$

$$\frac{\partial \Delta(v_x)}{\partial v_x} = (((v_x - ellip_x) \cdot \cos(\theta))' + (0-0) \cdot 0) + 0 + 0 - 1 \quad = \cos(\theta) - 1$$

$$\frac{\partial \Delta(v_x)}{\partial v_y} = \quad ((0-0) \cdot 0 + ((v_y - ellip_y) \cdot \sin(\theta))') + 0 + 0 - 0 = \sin(\theta)$$

$$\frac{\partial \Delta(v_y)}{\partial v_x} = (((v_x - ellip_x) \cdot (-\sin(\theta)))' + (0-0) \cdot 0) + 0 + 0 - 0 = -\sin(\theta)$$

$$\frac{\partial \Delta(v_y)}{\partial v_y} = ((0-0) \cdot (-0) + ((v_y - ellip_y) \cdot \cos(\theta))') + 0 + 0 - 1 = \cos(\theta) - 1$$

(12)

$$J_C = \begin{bmatrix} 1 + \cos(\theta) - 1 & 0 + \sin(\theta) \\ 0 - \sin(\theta) & 1 + \cos(\theta) - 1 \end{bmatrix}$$

$$J_C = \begin{bmatrix} \cos(\theta) & \sin(\theta) \\ -\sin(\theta) & \cos(\theta) \end{bmatrix}$$

(13)

Now we can put the formula (13) to (11) and deduce the final recurrent formula for the area C.

$$\begin{bmatrix} v_{x(i+1)} \\ v_{y(i+1)} \end{bmatrix} = \begin{bmatrix} v_{x(i)} \\ v_{y(i)} \end{bmatrix} - \left(\frac{1}{\cos^2(\theta) + \sin^2(\theta)} \cdot \begin{bmatrix} \cos(\theta) & -\sin(\theta) \\ \sin(\theta) & \cos(\theta) \end{bmatrix} \right) \cdot \begin{bmatrix} disto_x(v) \\ disto_y(v) \end{bmatrix}$$

$$\begin{bmatrix} v_{x(i+1)} \\ v_{y(i+1)} \end{bmatrix} = \begin{bmatrix} v_{x(i)} \\ v_{y(i)} \end{bmatrix} - \begin{bmatrix} \cos(\theta) & -\sin(\theta) \\ \sin(\theta) & \cos(\theta) \end{bmatrix} \cdot \begin{bmatrix} disto_x(v) \\ disto_y(v) \end{bmatrix}$$

$$\begin{bmatrix} v_{x(i+1)} \\ v_{y(i+1)} \end{bmatrix} = \begin{bmatrix} v_{x(i)} - (\cos(\theta) \cdot disto_x(v) - \sin(\theta) \cdot disto_y(v)) \\ v_{y(i)} - (\sin(\theta) \cdot disto_x(v) + \cos(\theta) \cdot disto_y(v)) \end{bmatrix}$$

(14)

The formula (14) can after some iteration come up with the inverted value for the pixel $(0, 0)^T$ in area C for any input values. We need to generalize that formula to invert any pixel in area C. Fortunately, that can be easily done by shifting the formula (14) by value of pixel we are inverting marked as $(v_{x0}, v_{y0})^T$. The final formula for the numerically inverting of any pixel of any input values in area C as it is in the method *AreaC_step*:

$$\begin{bmatrix} v_{x(i+1)} \\ v_{y(i+1)} \end{bmatrix} = \begin{bmatrix} v_{x(i)} - (\cos(\theta) \cdot (disto_x(v) - v_{x0}) - \sin(\theta) \cdot (disto_y(v) - v_{y0})) \\ v_{y(i)} - (\sin(\theta) \cdot (disto_x(v) - v_{x0}) + \cos(\theta) \cdot (disto_y(v) - v_{y0})) \end{bmatrix}$$

(15)

If **x** is in area B, than the evaluation of Jacobian matrix gets rather complicated. Thus for the inversion of all values in image we need to determine also J_B – Jacobian matrix for area B.

$$J_B = \begin{bmatrix} \dfrac{\partial v_x}{\partial v_x} + \dfrac{\partial(\Delta(v_x) \cdot coef\,(dist(\boldsymbol{v}), sp))}{\partial v_x} & \dfrac{\partial v_x}{\partial v_y} + \dfrac{\partial(\Delta(v_x) \cdot coef\,(dist(\boldsymbol{v}), sp))}{\partial v_y} \\[4mm] \dfrac{\partial v_y}{\partial v_x} + \dfrac{\partial(\Delta(v_y) \cdot coef\,(dist(\boldsymbol{v}), sp))}{\partial v_x} & \dfrac{\partial v_y}{\partial v_y} + \dfrac{\partial(\Delta(v_y) \cdot coef\,(dist(\boldsymbol{v}), sp))}{\partial v_y} \end{bmatrix}$$

To ensure a higher readability each element of the matrix J_B will be discussed separately, their labels are:

$$J_B = \begin{bmatrix} j_{b1} & j_{b2} \\ j_{b3} & j_{b4} \end{bmatrix}$$

$$j_{b1} = 1 + \frac{\partial \Delta(v_x)}{\partial v_x} \cdot coef\,(dist(\boldsymbol{v}), sp) + \Delta(v_x) \frac{\partial\, coef\,(dist(\boldsymbol{v}), sp)}{\partial v_x}$$

$$j_{b2} = 0 + \frac{\partial \Delta(v_x)}{\partial v_y} \cdot coef\,(dist(\boldsymbol{v}), sp) + \Delta(v_x) \frac{\partial\, coef\,(dist(\boldsymbol{v}), sp)}{\partial v_y}$$

$$j_{b3} = 0 + \frac{\partial \Delta(v_y)}{\partial v_x} \cdot coef\,(dist(\boldsymbol{v}), sp) + \Delta(v_y) \frac{\partial\, coef\,(dist(\boldsymbol{v}), sp)}{\partial v_x} \qquad (16)$$

$$j_{b4} = 1 + \frac{\partial \Delta(v_y)}{\partial v_y} \cdot coef\,(dist(\boldsymbol{v}), sp) + \Delta(v_y) \frac{\partial\, coef\,(dist(\boldsymbol{v}), sp)}{\partial v_y}$$

As we can see, to evaluate these elements we need to find out partial derivatives of the function Δ from the formula (12) and partial derivatives of the function *coef*.

$$\frac{\partial\, coef\,(dist(\boldsymbol{v}), sp)}{\partial v_x} = \frac{1}{2}\left(1 - \cos\left(\frac{dist(\boldsymbol{v}) \cdot \pi}{sp}\right)\right)' =$$

$$= \frac{1}{2}\left(-\cos'\left(\frac{dist(\boldsymbol{v}) \cdot \pi}{sp}\right) \cdot \left(\frac{dist(\boldsymbol{v}) \cdot \pi}{sp}\right)'\right) =$$

$$\frac{1}{2}\left(\sin\left(\frac{dist(\boldsymbol{v}) \cdot \pi}{sp}\right) \cdot \left(\frac{(dist(\boldsymbol{v}) \cdot \pi)' \cdot sp}{sp^2}\right)\right) = \frac{1}{2}\left(\sin\left(\frac{dist(\boldsymbol{v}) \cdot \pi}{sp}\right) \cdot \left(\frac{dist(\boldsymbol{v})' \cdot \pi \cdot sp}{sp^2}\right)\right)$$

From the last result we can see that the derivation of coefficient is the same for ∂x and ∂y and it is:

$$\frac{\partial\, coef\,(dist(\boldsymbol{v}), sp)}{\partial v_x} = \frac{\partial\, coef\,(dist(\boldsymbol{v}), sp)}{\partial v_y} = \frac{1}{2}\left(\sin\left(\frac{dist(\boldsymbol{v}) \pi}{sp}\right)\left(\frac{dist(\boldsymbol{v})' \pi}{sp}\right)\right)$$

$$(17)$$

But we still need to compute the derivation of the function *dist*.

$$\frac{\partial \, dist(\boldsymbol{v})}{\partial v_x} = \left(\frac{(v_x - ellip_x)^2}{semi_x^2} + \frac{(v_y - ellip_y)^2}{semi_y^2} \right)^{\frac{1}{2}}{}' =$$

$$= \frac{1}{2} \left(\frac{1}{\sqrt{\dfrac{(v_x - ellip_x)^2}{semi_x^2} + \dfrac{(v_y - ellip_y)^2}{semi_y^2}}} \right) \left(\frac{(v_x - ellip_x)^2}{semi_x^2} + \frac{(v_y - ellip_y)^2}{semi_y^2} \right)' =$$

$$\frac{\partial \, dist(\boldsymbol{v})}{\partial v_x} = \frac{1}{2} \frac{1}{\sqrt{\dfrac{(v_x - ellip_x)^2}{semi_x^2} + \dfrac{(v_y - ellip_y)^2}{semi_y^2}}} \left(\frac{(v_x - ellip_x)^2{}' \cdot semi_x^2}{semi_x^4} \right) \quad (18)$$

$$\frac{\partial \, dist(\boldsymbol{v})}{\partial v_x} = \frac{1}{2} \left(\frac{\dfrac{2(v_x - ellip_x)}{semi_x^2}}{\sqrt{\dfrac{(v_x - ellip_x)^2}{semi_x^2} + \dfrac{(v_y - ellip_y)^2}{semi_y^2}}} \right)$$

$$\frac{\partial \, dist(\boldsymbol{v})}{\partial v_x} = \frac{(v_x - ellip_x)}{semi_x^2 \cdot \sqrt{\dfrac{(v_x - ellip_x)^2}{semi_x^2} + \dfrac{(v_y - ellip_y)^2}{semi_y^2}}} \quad (19)$$

The only difference in computing partial derivatives of function *dist* with respect to v_y is in the last step in the formula (18). Without inferencing again there is the result:

$$\frac{\partial \, dist(\boldsymbol{v})}{\partial v_y} = \frac{(v_y - ellip_y)}{semi_y^2 \cdot \sqrt{\dfrac{(v_x - ellip_x)^2}{semi_x^2} + \dfrac{(v_y - ellip_y)^2}{semi_y^2}}} \quad (20)$$

Now it is possible to complete the formula (17) for partial derivatives by the substitution of the results in the formula (19) and (20).

$$\frac{\partial \, coef(dist(\boldsymbol{v}), sp)}{\partial v_x} =$$

$$\frac{1}{2}\left(\sin\left(\frac{dist(\boldsymbol{v})\cdot\pi}{sp}\right)\cdot\left(\frac{\dfrac{(v_x-ellip_x)}{semi_x^2\cdot\sqrt{\dfrac{(v_x-ellip_x)^2}{semi_x^2}+\dfrac{(v_y-ellip_y)^2}{semi_y^2}}}\cdot\pi}{sp}\right)\right)=$$

$$\frac{\partial\,coef\,(dist(\boldsymbol{v}),sp)}{\partial v_x}=\frac{\sin\left(\dfrac{dist(\boldsymbol{v})\cdot\pi}{sp}\right)\cdot(v_x-ellip_x)\cdot\pi}{2\cdot sp\cdot semi_x^2\cdot\sqrt{\dfrac{(v_x-ellip_x)^2}{semi_x^2}+\dfrac{(v_y-ellip_y)^2}{semi_y^2}}} \qquad (21)$$

$$\frac{\partial\,coef\,(dist(\boldsymbol{v}),sp)}{\partial v_y}=\frac{\sin\left(\dfrac{dist(\boldsymbol{v})\cdot\pi}{sp}\right)\cdot(v_y-ellip_y)\cdot\pi}{2\cdot sp\cdot semi_y^2\cdot\sqrt{\dfrac{(v_x-ellip_x)^2}{semi_x^2}+\dfrac{(v_y-ellip_y)^2}{semi_y^2}}} \qquad (22)$$

Formula (21) and (22) are represented by the method *D_koef*. Partial derivatives of the function *coef* and Δ in formulas (21), (22), (12) can be now substituted to the formula (16) of elements of Jacobian matrix for area B J_B. In the result there are no ways to reduce the complexity so for the sake of readability the final formula stays in the format without substitution and uses labelling from the formula (16). We use Jacobian matrix J_B in the formula (11) to get the recurrent formula:

$$\begin{bmatrix} v_{x(i+1)} \\ v_{y(i+1)} \end{bmatrix}=\begin{bmatrix} v_{x(i)} \\ v_{y(i)} \end{bmatrix}-\left(\frac{1}{b_{j1}b_{j4}-b_{j2}b_{j3}}\cdot\begin{bmatrix} b_{j4} & -b_{j2} \\ -b_{j3} & b_{j1} \end{bmatrix}\right)\cdot\begin{bmatrix} disto_x(\boldsymbol{v}) \\ disto_y(\boldsymbol{v}) \end{bmatrix}$$

As in the formula (15) also for this formula to work properly on any input pixels we need to add shifting parameters $(v_{x\,0}, v_{y\,0})^T$ which denote coordinates from which we are finding the inverse value.

$$\begin{bmatrix} v_{x(i+1)} \\ v_{y(i+1)} \end{bmatrix}=\begin{bmatrix} v_{x(i)}-\left(\dfrac{b_{j4}(disto_x(\boldsymbol{v})-v_{x0})}{b_{j1}b_{j4}-b_{j2}b_{j3}}-\dfrac{b_{j2}(disto_y(\boldsymbol{v})-v_{y0})}{b_{j1}b_{j4}-b_{j2}b_{j3}}\right) \\ v_{y(i)}-\left(\dfrac{-b_{j3}(disto_x(\boldsymbol{v})-v_{x0})}{b_{j1}b_{j4}-b_{j2}b_{j3}}+\dfrac{b_{j1}(disto_y(\boldsymbol{v})-v_{y0})}{b_{j1}b_{j4}-b_{j2}b_{j3}}\right) \end{bmatrix} \qquad (23)$$

The formula (23) with the substituted function Δ from the formula (16) corresponds with the method *AreaB_step*. The method *NewtonRaphson_step* just chooses the right area step method and uses it. Each numerical method must have an ending condition. The method *Precision* computes the following formula and when this condition is satisfied, it ends iterations.

$$|v_{x(i+1)} - v_{xi}| < 0.0001 \quad \wedge \quad |v_{y(i+1)} - v_{yi}| < 0.0001$$

As it experimentally shows up, although that method should be by [18] convergent, it sometimes cycles between some solutions. To prevent this behaviour after 100 iteration it does 10 more and uses the best solution so far (the best is one with the smallest cumulative error when computing the inverted value back using the original model). All these fixed values can be changed.

After this it is finally possible to use the interpolation to approximate the value that should be in this point. For this purpose the bilinear interpolation is used. The basic formula for this interpolation of point (v_x, v_y) (v_x, v_y can be in this case real numbers), is [19]:

$$intensity(v_x, v_y) = (1-t)(1-u)i_1 + t(1-u)i_2 + tui_3 + (1-t)ui_4$$
$$i_1 = intensity(x_{low}, y_{low})$$
$$i_2 = intensity(x_{low}+1, y_{low})$$
$$i_3 = intensity(x_{low}+1, y_{low}+1)$$
$$i_4 = intensity(x_{low}, y_{low}+1)$$

Where x_{low} and y_{low} are integer parts of numbers v_x and v_y respectively. Because pixels of the original image are creating a uniform square grid we can use a simplified definition of values $\underline{t}$ and $\underline{u}$. Values $\underline{t}$ and $\underline{u}$ are fractional parts of numbers v_x and v_y. After the interpolation of all marked points, the distortion is done.

As an extension two checkboxes are used. One for the preview of areas which create the image as it is shown in figure 4.1. The method *Preview* does not compute the model, it only graphically shows the individual areas with the original fingerprint image as a background. As we know from the previous paragraphs, the pixel coordinates are integers but the model returns real numbers. To achieve a more precise distortion it is better to use the interpolation to all points of the image (with exception of that in area A). However, the computing of inverted values and the interpolation takes time so this fully interpolated variant is slower than the applied model which interpolates only the needed points. In conclusion, the method *applyDmg* is, according to used checkboxes, calling the method *Preview* or calling *applyModel* and then *applyInterpolation* or after marking of all points in areas B and C calling only the method *applyInterpolation*. The method *applyModel* uses just the formulas (1), (2), (6), (7) and (5) to all points of the image. The undistorted points are marked and interpolated by calling the method applyInterpolation. The method *applyInterpolation* uses *NewtonRaphson_step* until the method *Precision* returns true and interpolates the previous results for each marked point.

6 Verification of Damaged Fingerprints

This chapter is dealing with the verification of the resulting images. Firstly, it will be verified that each type of damage is simulating a real damage. Factors influencing fingerprint images usually do not have precise mathematical models, that means that their verification is difficult and can be done only based on the similarities with real fingerprints. However, fingerprint databases normally do not contain severely damaged fingerprints images. These are deleted in time of the fingerprint acquisition and they are replaced with less damaged ones. The goal of this work was not to perfectly simulate damage done on the given fingerprint image but to simulate a real damage to some extent. In the second part this exactly will be evaluated, that means it will be stated how much damage was done to the perfect fingerprint not only with one damage but with a combination of all of them.

6.1 Verification of Individual Damage Simulation

As it was said the individual damage verification will be based on real fingerprint images. If it is not told otherwise, all images are from the fingerprint database made in cooperation with doctoral students in Brno University of Technology. Optical and

Figure 6.1: Real (left) and simulated (right) fingerprint from damaged sensor.

capacitive sensors were chosen as a source of images. It is because they are the most commonly used and there are many databases using these technologies. Note that touch or area sensors were used.

Firstly, the simulation of damaged sensor will be described. On the left side in figure 6.1 there is a real acquired fingerprint image and on the right there is a simulated one. We can see that there is a crack in the protective glass on the left bottom side of the image and there is also a small crack on the right bottom side. The left side crack is simulated in the right image. We can see that the real crack is in a slightly different angle but otherwise the thickness and location are very real looking.

Using the same damage simulation we can also achieve the simulation of dirt on the sensor. As it is not the main purpose of this damage simulation, it is usually necessary to use it several times to achieve the simulation of dirt on the sensor. Real images in figure 6.2 are from [11] where it is stated that oiled finger and hair on the sensor leave similar mark on the fingerprint image. In figure 6.2 we can see oiled fingerprint image on the left, hair on the sensor in the centre (this image is from the thermal sensor) and fingerprint from application.

Figure 6.2: Real fingerprint images – oiled finger, hair on the sensor and simulated synthetic image.

Second, the simulation of pressure and dampness will be discussed. Morphological operations used to simulate this kind of damage do by definition the same damage like high pressure or moisture. They are thickening or thinning all lines in image so if they are used as the first kind of damage they do exactly the same thing like this influential factor. In figure 6.3 we can see in the first row real fingerprint images from high pressure to low pressure. In the same figure we see in the second row synthetic images in the same order.

Figure 6.3: Real and synthetic fingerprint images with different levels of pressure and moisture.

Finally the last type of simulated damage is discussed, that is the fingerprint distortion. It is the only simulated damage that is following a verified mathematical model (which is described in [15]). Also it is the only damage that is very difficult to see. It is possible to find in the literature [3] [15] images of distorted and non-distorted fingerprints where few minutia are highlighted but even then the difference between them is not obvious. Instead you can see in figure 6.4 distorted and non-distorted synthetic fingerprints images and the comparison with regular square grid instead. In the first row there are non-distorted images (synthetic normal, square grid, square grid fully interpolated and synthetic fully interpolated) and in the second row there are distorted images in the same order.

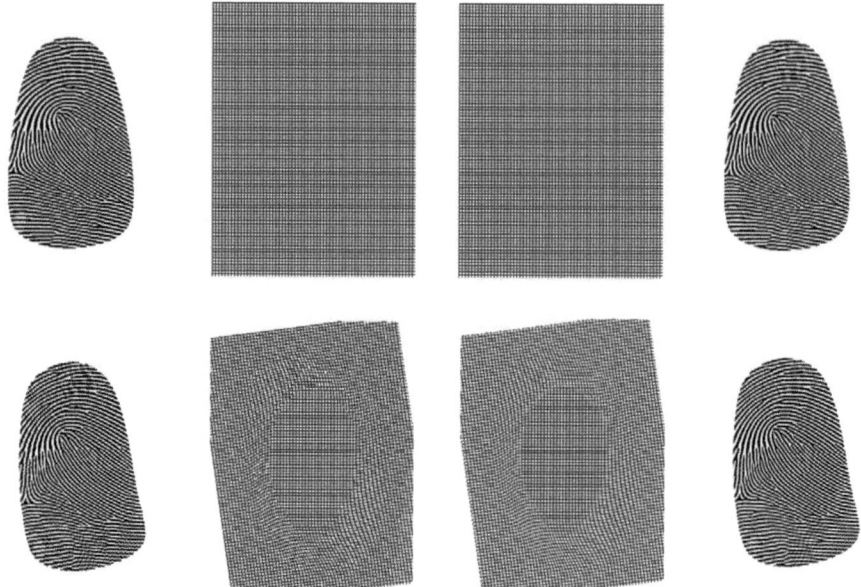

Figure 6.4: Non-distorted (up) and distorted (down) interpolated (left) and fully interpolated (right) synthetic fingerprint images.

6.2   Verification of Resulting Fingerprints

In this chapter the final images are tested. All damage simulations are used not only individually but with all possible combinations. They are used in specific order and all images have a unique name by this pattern. The prefix SFP (synthetic fingerprint) is followed by a sequence number and then zero or more suffixes determining the used damage simulations. The order of simulations and abbreviation for them are: pressure and moisture (pm), fingerprint distortion (dis), dirt on the sensor (dir) and damaged sensor (dmg). Perfect synthetic fingerprints were generated by SFinGe 4.1st version. After the consultation with the supervisor these fingerprints were damaged with these input values. Pressure and moisture uses the level two dilatation. The fingerprint distortion uses normal interpolation, skin elasticity 1.0, rotation angle 8°, translation in axis x 6 pixels and translation in axis y 3 pixels. The dirt on the sensor uses a thicker line, length 7, angle 0° and starting point (x,y) = (90, 120). The damaged sensor uses length 10, angle 90° and starting point (220, 330). For better idea how fingerprint images used for testing look like see figures 6.3 upper right image (perfect fingerprint), 6.3 bottom right image (pm), 6.4 bottom left image (dis), 6.2 and 6.1 right images (dir and dmg). These figures are using the same input values as the images used for testing.

For verification two methods were used. The first method is using the commercial software Neurotechnology VeriFinger 6.2 where the score between the perfect fingerprint and all associated impressions was made. The second method is the value of fingerprint quality by the software NBIS release 4.2.0, specifically the program *nfiq* in release 4.1.0 which is the implementation of the standard ANSI/NIST-ITL 1-2007. 40 perfect synthetic fingerprints were generated for testing. When generating these test fingerprints, the probabilistic distribution of the classes of the fingerprints was taken into account.

Score in Neurotechnology software is not expressed in percent but with a specific number. To compare the damage simulations the score between perfect fingerprint image and the same image was found out and then designated to 100%. The score of other simulations is relative to this identity score. Because the database with the score is large, only the statistical result for the simulations will be presented.

Chart 6.1: Relative score from VeriFinger.

	Average	Maximum	Minimum
SFPx	100,00%	100,00%	100,00%
SFPx_dir	99,32%	121,78%	91,41%
SFPx_dis	53,77%	77,55%	31,66%
SFPx_dmg	95,05%	101,91%	84,36%
SFPx_pm	61,34%	95,50%	35,15%
SFPx_dir_dmg	94,82%	119,62%	81,64%
SFPx_dis_dir	53,27%	76,74%	30,17%
SFPx_dis_dmg	53,17%	77,77%	29,94%
SFPx_pm_dir	61,32%	95,38%	33,75%
SFPx_pm_dis	37,57%	63,94%	17,94%
SFPx_pm_dmg	59,85%	83,85%	37,25%
SFPx_dis_dir_dmg	52,83%	76,95%	29,03%
SFPx_pm_dir_dmg	59,62%	83,85%	35,88%
SFPx_pm_dis_dir	36,54%	64,13%	0,00%
SFPx_pm_dis_dmg	37,64%	65,35%	15,84%
SFPx_pm_dis_dir_dmg	36,99%	65,24%	13,90%

As we can see in chart 6.1 the most successful damage on its own is the fingerprint distortion. The combination of pressure and moisture and distortion is the best damage simulation based on this statistic. The exception in the minimum column is because software said that quality of the fingerprint image (SFP40_pm_dis_dir) is too low, so for this one image the result is 0%. Another extreme result is the maximum of SFP23_dir which is possibly because of false minutiae caused by the simulation. That is the only explanation why this fingerprint is in terms of score exceeding the original.

The evaluation of fingerprint images by the *nfiq* application assigns to the fingerprint image a quality grade from 1 to 5, where 1 is the best quality and 5 is the worst. *Nfiq* determines these grades by computing the feature vector that contains

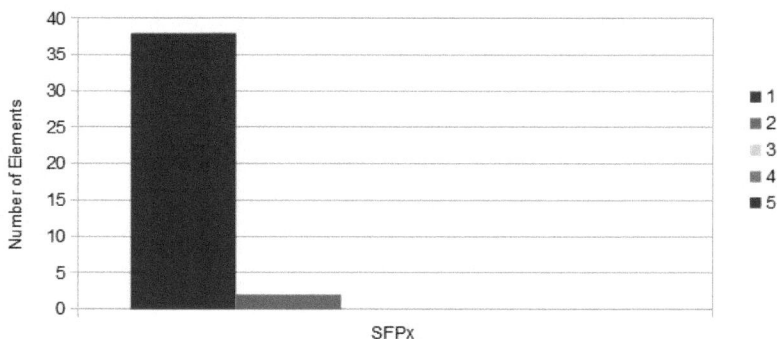

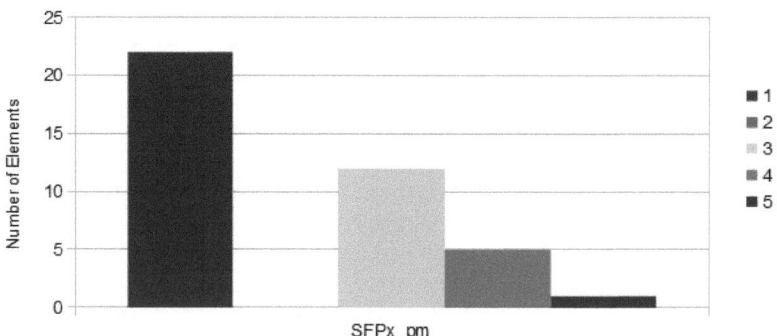

Figure 6.5: Histograms of the fingerprint image quality representatives.

foreground, total number of minutia, several number of minutiae that have various quality and percentages of the foreground blocks with various quality, as it is described in [20]. To do that it needs strictly 8bit colour depth. Because of that all the greyscale images with 24bit colour depth were converted to 8bit colour depth. After the evaluation of all fingerprint images and processing of all feature vectors and the final image quality, it shows up that the distribution of data is not normal. Almost no images have the quality of two. Because of that it is not possible to use standard statistic tools like median. When we look at the histogram of fingerprint image quality in appendix A, we can see two patterns. To show them two representatives were chosen and their histogram is shown in figure 6.5. As we can see the images damaged by pressure and moisture have a great impact on the final score.

To see exactly which damage simulation has the greatest impact on the final grade we compute the quantile of grade 3 or worse. The results are shown in chart 6.2.

Chart 6.2: Quantile of the grades 3 or worse.

	Quantile of 3 to 5
SFPx	0,0%
SFPx_dir	0,0%
SFPx_dis	2,5%
SFPx_dmg	0,0%
SFPx_pm	45,0%
SFPx_dir_dmg	0,0%
SFPx_dis_dir	2,5%
SFPx_dis_dmg	2,5%
SFPx_pm_dir	45,0%
SFPx_pm_dis	40,0%
SFPx_pm_dmg	42,5%
SFPx_dis_dir_dmg	5,0%
SFPx_pm_dir_dmg	42,5%
SFPx_pm_dis_dir	37,5%
SFPx_pm_dis_dmg	40,0%
SFPx_pm_dis_dir_dmg	35,0%

As it was expected from the histogram, pressure and moisture have the highest influence on the image quality score. Papillary lines clarity and thickness are one of the metrics that are used to evaluate the fingerprint image quality and that is why pressure and moisture have such a huge effect.

To sum everything up, both tests show that the biggest influential factors implemented are the pressure and the moisture. The fingerprint distortion is the second most influential. It is certain that the pressure and the dampness damage fingerprint image quality while the fingerprint distortion does almost no damage at all. The fingerprint distortion only moves some minutiae but does not worsen the quality of them. On the other hand, when it comes to the comparison between the original fingerprint and his impression, fingerprint distortion, as it was shown in the first test, was more successful. The impression of a given fingerprint using both these methods shows that its score when it comes to verification based on the perfect fingerprint is about 62,5% lower and the impression on its own is about one class of the fingerprint image quality worse. This results shows that the original fingerprint is clearly damaged by the implemented application, which was the goal of this work.

7 Conclusion

This work is covering the state of the art of fingerprint acquirement and recognition. Also methods of generating the synthetic fingerprint and the fingerprint reconstruction are described. This description was focused on the SFinGe generator and its methods. There are listed supposedly all phenomena that can damage the image of fingerprint created by a biometric device. From them I have chosen pressure and moisture, dirt on the sensor, damaged sensor and fingerprint distortion. I have designed and have implemented methods for the simulation of their influence on the final fingerprint image.

Despite of the existence of the application SFinGe I designed my application to be more sensors oriented and expandable. This design allows not only to determine magnitude of influential factors but also to closely specify the sensor and its type and adapt the damage simulation to it. This way it can better simulate the specific conditions. After testing all combinations of the damage simulation on 40 synthetic fingerprints it is discovered that the best results are achieved with the combination of fingerprint distortion, pressure and moisture. This combination has 62.5% worse score in commercial product than the original image and it is one fingerprint image quality class worse (20%) when testing according to the standard ANSI/NIST-ITL 1-2007.

The design of this application was made with the intention of extending this application. There are many phenomena that can be simulated and also many sensors that can partially influence damage simulation. As a future work there is a lot of space for improvement. The fingerprint generator can be improved to allow to define the fingerprint class or to specify the location of singularities. This way it should create more realistic fingerprints. Also when other sensors come to mind, the generator could be modified to create the fingerprint from different sensors. Existing damage simulations, especially the simulation of pressure, can be optimized to work faster. The fingerprint distortion can in cooperation with the location of singularities approximate the centre of fingerprint more precisely. New damage simulation can be introduced, for example noising which simulates various smaller factors and simulation of fingerprint background which is very sensor dependent. A big challenge would be the simulation of sweeping sensors which has never been done before.

When we look at the whole publication, in chapter 2 the methods of fingerprint recognition and the basic knowledge needed to understand them are covered. In chapter 3 the synthetic fingerprint generators are discussed. Among discussed generators there are the methods used by SFinGe of University of Bologna and the Chaloupka's generator described in his master's thesis named Fingerprint generator. In chapters 4 and 5 some methods of the intentional damage of quality of fingerprint was chosen. These methods were designed and implemented to the Chaloupka's fingerprint generator with respect of modularity. Chapter 6 proves that they are significantly damaging the original synthetic fingerprint image. In addition the basic batch processing and some optional features to the implemented damage simulation were made.

Bibliography

[1] *Internation standard ISO/IEC 2382-37 Information technology -- Vocabulary -- Part 37: Biometrics.* 2012.

[2] Drahanský, M., Orság, F. et al.: *Biometrie.* Computer Press a.s., 2011, pages 294. ISBN 978-80-254-8979-6.

[3] Maltoni, D., Maio, D., Jain, A.K. and Prabhakar, S.: *Handbook of Fingerprint Recognition.* Springer, 2009, pages 512. ISBN 978-1-8488-2254-2.

[4] Jain, A.K., Bolle, R., Pankanti, S. et al.: *Biometrics: Personal Identification in Networked Society.* Kluwer Academic Publications, 1999, pages 411. ISBN 978-0-7923-8345-1.

[5] Drahanský, M.: *Fingerprint Recognition Technology - Related Topics.* LAP LAMBERT Academic Publishing GmbH & Co. KG, 2011, pages 172. ISBN 978-3-8443-3007-6.

[6] Chaloupka, R.: *Generátor otisků prstů.* Brno, 2007. diplomová práce. FIT VUT v Brně.

[7] Federal Bureau of Investigation: *Integrated Automated Fingerprint Identification System - Web page* [online]. 2014. [cit. 2014-5-21]. Avaiable from: http://www.fbi.gov/about-us/cjis/fingerprints_biometrics/iafis

[8] Drahanský, M.: *Biometric Systems*, Course at the Faculty of Information Technology, BUT, http://www.fit.vutbr.cz/study/courses/BIO/.

[9] Zhao, Q., Jain, A.K., Paulter, N.G., Taylor, M.: *Fingerprint image synthesis based on statistical feature models*, 2012 IEEE Fifth International Conference on Biometrics: Theory, Applications and Systems (BTAS), pages 23-30, ISBN 978-14-673-1384-1, URL: http://ieeexplore.ieee.org/stamp/stamp.jsp?tp=&arnumber=6374554&isnumber=6374538.

[10] Cappelli, R.: *SFinGe: an Approach to Synthetic Fingerprint Generation*, In BT 2004 - International Workshop on Biometric Technologies. Calgary, Canada: 2004, pages 147-154.

[11] Tuč, D.: *Testing of the Environmental Influences on Fingerprints Sensors*. Brno, 2005. bachelor project. FIT BUT in Brno.

[12] University of Bologna: *Biometric System Laboratory - Web page* [online]. 2014 [cit. 2014-1-13]. Avaiable from: http://biolab.csr.unibo.it/research.asp.

[13] Cappelli, R., Maio, D., Maltoni, D.: *Synthetic Fingerprint-Database Generation*, 16th International Conference on Pattern Recognition (ICPR2002), Québec City, Canada: 2002, pages 744-747. ISBN 0-7695-1695-X

[14] Gonzalez, R.C., Woods, R.E.:: *Digital Image Processing (3rd Edition)*. Prentice Hall, 2008, pages 954. ISBN 978-0-1316-8728-8.

[15] Singh, S., Murshed, N., Kropatsch, W.: *Modelling Plastic Distortion in Fingerprint Images*, Second Internation Conference on Advances in Pattern Recognition (ICAPR2001), Rio de Janiero, Brazil: 2001, pages 369-376. ISBN 3-540-41767-2

[16] Pecinovský, R.: *Návrhové vzory*. Computer Press, 2007, pages 528. ISBN 978-80-251-1582-4.

[17] Ralston, A.: *Základy numerické matematiky*. Academia, Praha: 1973, pages 636.

[18] Haluzíková, A.: *Numerické metody*. Vysoké učení technické v Čs.redakci VM MON, 1989, pages 124. ISBN 80-214-0039-0.

[19] Press, W.H., Teukolsky, S.A., Vetterling, W.T., Flannery, B.P.: *Numerical Recipes in C: The Art of Scientific Computing (2nd edition)*, Cambridge University Press, Cambridge: 2002, pages 925. ISBN 0-521-43108-5

[20] Tabassi, E., Wilson, C.L., Watson, C.I.: *Fingerprint Image Quality*, NISTIR 7151, National Institute of Standards and Technology, pages 72, 2004.

Appendix A Fingerprint Image Quality Histogram

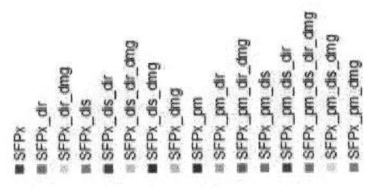

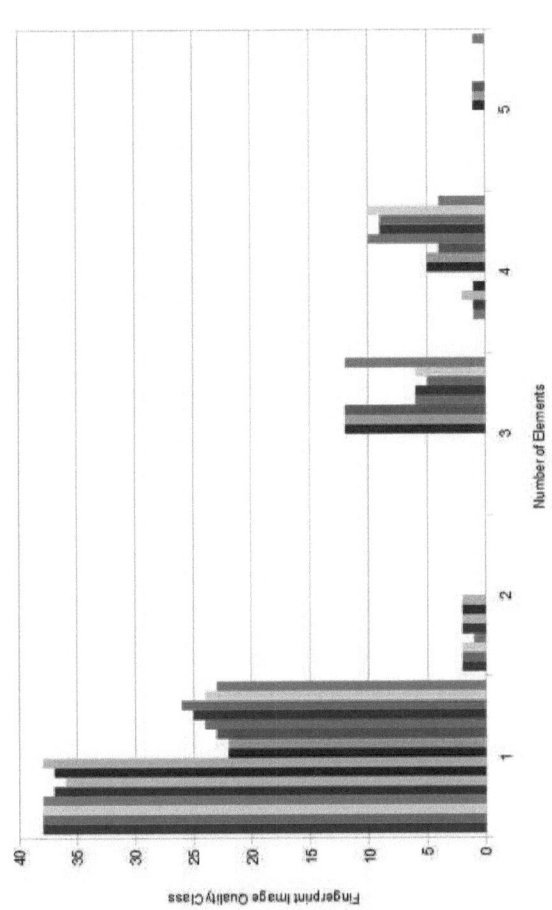

Printed by Books on Demand GmbH, Norderstedt / Germany